Technology Choice
in Developing Countries

Technology Choice in Developing Countries
The Textile and Pulp and Paper Industries

Michel A. Amsalem

The MIT Press
Cambridge, Massachusetts
London, England

This book was set in Palatino by The MIT Press Computergraphics Department and printed and bound by Halliday Lithograph in the United States of America.

Library of Congress Cataloging in Publication Data

Amsalem, Michael A.
    Technology choice in developing countries.

    Bibliography: p.
    Includes index.
    1. Underdeveloped areas—Economic policy. 2. Underdeveloped areas—Technology—Social aspects. 3. Underdeveloped areas—Paper making and trade. 4. Underdeveloped areas—Textile industry. I. Title.
HC59.7.A778 1983   338.9′009172′4   82-17918
ISBN 0-262-01072-0

To my parents

Contents

List of Tables

List of Figures

Acknowledgments

A book based on field research requires the collaboration of so many people that it would be impossible to acknowledge my debt to each one of them. Furthermore, the invaluable help I received from each of the corporations was supplied with the understanding that its source would remain anonymous. My debt to the managers and engineers of the textile producers, the pulp and paper producers and the equipment suppliers interviewed is, however, too great not to be acknowledged at least in a general way.

I also want to express my gratitude to Professor Robert B. Stobaugh, Professor Raymond Vernon, and Professor Louis T. Wells, Jr., who guided me, advised me, and on occasion prodded me when my energies were faltering. I found their comments on every draft of this book to be incisive and stimulating. They greatly contributed to the final product of this research effort.

This study would not have been possible without the financial support of the International Finance Corporation (World Bank Group). Its contribution was not limited to the cost of the field research, since it generously provided me with contacts, logistical support, and advice. My special thanks go to Dr. Moeen A. Qureshi and Dr. Dale R. Weigel who, besides being responsible for much of the support this organization lent me, also added some of their own. I should stress that even though this book benefited from numerous discussions with World Bank staff, the views expressed and the conclusions reached are the sole responsibility of its author and should not be taken to represent World Bank policies or opinions.

Ms. Christine Masi, Ms. Vimla Moses, Mr. Morris Rabinko, and Ms. Phyllis Weatherly managed to keep an even temper and pleasant disposition through numerous drafts and unending changes.

I have a very special debt towards my close friend Mr. Brian W. Berman, who not only helped me through sometimes discouraging dealings with electronic data processing, but also provided constant moral support and always made himsellf available when I felt the need to discuss ideas or analytical points.

Last but not least is my gratitude to Tammy, my wife. Life through successive deadlines and the anguish associated with all that can go wrong in an empirical study put tremendous pressures on her. But as if withstanding all of these pressures was not enough of a contribution, she took on a much larger burden, helped me through all of the drafts, played a major role in the successive editings, discussed with me every point. Without her support and her help this book would never have seen the light of day.

Technology Choice
in Developing Countries

1   The Choice-of-Technology Issue and This Study

Every year developing countries must create more than 50 million new jobs merely to prevent their levels of unemployment and underemployment from worsening. Physical limitations and already high rates of underemployment restrict the potential for job creation in agriculture. The service sector is also overcrowded, and productive employment can be expected to grow only slowly. This leaves manufacturing as the single potential source for most of the new jobs that must be generated. Given the present cost of creating a manufacturing job, however, this sector will be able to absorb only a fraction of the new entrants into the labor force at present investment levels.

Faced with such alarming prospects, developing countries have been searching for policies that will lead to significant increases in the creation of employment. Lowering the investment cost per job created is one of the most obvious ways to achieve that aim. It seems reasonable that given the developing countries' relative abundance of labor and scarcity of capital, they would use technologies that require little capital and large amounts of labor for the production of a given good.[1]

This idea, however, has provoked one of the greatest controversies in the field of economic development. Although the subject of much research and argumentation, the basic questions concerning the potential for substituting labor for capital in manufacturing remain unanswered. Little consensus has been reached on the existence of labor-intensive technologies or the potential benefits to be drawn from their application. Further disputes exist about the extent to which these technologies are already in use in developing countries, the reasons why they may or may not be adopted by manufacturing facilities, and the means by which their wider adoption could be promoted.

This study investigates the following issues:
- Are alternative technologies available to perform a specific manufacturing operation? Do these alternative technologies use the factors of production in significantly different proportions?
- How do the technologies adopted by manufacturing firms in developing countries compare with the alternatives available in terms of quantity of the different factors of production required?
- What are the considerations that lead a firm to adopt a specific technology rather than alternatives? And how do these considerations enter the decision process?

These issues are addressed by means of a comprehensive survey of the offerings of pulp and paper and textile equipment suppliers and a detailed analysis of the technology choices made for production facilities in developing countries. The relevance of this work should not be limited to these two industries, however. The system of analysis of technology choices developed here can be applied to other industries to provide answers to the same questions. This methodology can also be used by firms to evaluate alternative technologies and by governments to assess the impact of proposed policies on technology choice. Furthermore from the findings in this inquiry, preliminary conclusions can be reached regarding the form and characteristics of alternative technologies available in different types of industries, the selection behavior of specific types of firms, and the impact on technology choice of specific government policies.

The Controversy about Technology Choice

Economists and policy makers not only accept the questions addressed here as relevant but also as crucial to the issue of technology choice. But there the consensus ends, however, and there has been little agreement about the answers to these questions. A rapid review of the main schools of thought will show the scope of the controversy.

The Existence of a Range of Alternative Technologies

This is the premise on which the notion of technology choice rests. For technology choice to be a relevant issue, there needs to be a range of alternative technologies available to produce a specific good at a given scale of production. Furthermore these technologies have to make use of the factors of production in proportions different enough for the choice among them to have a significant impact on the demand for these factors.

The controversy about technology choice also begins at this juncture. So little information has been collected about the availability and characteristics of alternative technologies for the production of a given good that the most contradictory positions still coexist on this issue. Neoclassical economic theory assumes the existence of an infinite number of alternative technologies available for the production of any good at any scale. It also assumes that these alternative technologies create a continuum along which it is possible to substitute one factor of production for another. Others argue that there are no alternative technologies and consequently that there is no choice for a rational decision maker. According to them one technology—generally the most modern one—uses both less labor and less capital than the other and, being altogether more efficient, should always be preferred.

Characteristics of the Technologies Adopted

If there is a range of alternative technologies for the production of a given good at a specific scale of manufacturing, one should then wonder what the characteristics of the technologies chosen are as compared to the characteristics of the alternatives. Since the emphasis in the technology choice issue is on the quantity of the different factors of production that may be put to use by alternative technologies, this should be the criterion used to compare the technology that is chosen against its alternatives.

Neoclassical economic theory posits that the play of market forces should result in a pricing of the factors of production such that the technology using these factors of production in a proportion closest to their relative availability in the economy should yield the lowest cost of production. Therefore a rational decision maker, whose aim is the minimization of production costs, should always choose this technology. If chosen by all production units in the country, these technologies should result in the full use of the factors of production. In other words the adoption of such technologies should lead, among other things, to full employment.

Although from a logical point of view, the neoclassical theory of technology choice is unassailable, a cursory review of the employment situation in developing countries indicates the theory's incapacity to explain actual conditions in these countries. Most developing countries are plagued by constant unemployment and underemployment, a situation that cannot be reconciled with neoclassical theory.[2] Several arguments have been advanced to explain this discrepancy, but the accumulated empirical evidence has not allowed a testing of the different explanations offered.

Three main lines of explanation exist for the failure of technology choice to lead to full employment of the factors of production beside the above-mentioned argument of technological fixity (the absence of alternatives). One concentrates on the link between factor availability and factor prices. Market imperfections and government intervention, its proponents contend, result in factor prices that do not correspond to the relative availability of these factors.[3] Private decision makers may well choose the cost-minimizing technology, but since this is based on prices that do not reflect the availability of the factors, full employment of the factors of production will not result. Therefore the factor price determination mechanisms, not the technology choice procedures, are at fault.

Another explanation stresses the limitations of a two-factor model of technology choice. It notes that the labor factor of production includes unskilled, semiskilled, skilled, supervisory, and managerial employees, while the capital factor of production is made up of both local currency and foreign exchange. Furthermore alternative technologies might also differ in their use of some other inputs such as power, raw materials, and chemicals. Under such circumstances it is highly unlikely that a technology can be found that will use all of the factors of production and inputs in proportions equal to their relative availability. The technologies chosen, although cost minimizing among the sets of available alternatives, might therefore still lead to the underemployment of some factors of production.

The third explanation questions the mechanism that the neoclassical theorists assume to be the one that leads to technology choices. Production cost minimization, the countertheorists argue, is not the ultimate objective of the decision maker in choosing a technology. This is because imperfect markets and product differentiation allow firms to escape price competition. Since they are not under pressure to minimize their firm's cost of production, these managers will try to satisfy other objectives. In that event, for example, minimization of the risk associated with the use of untried alternatives and reinforcement of the stability of an oligopoly will become decisive factors in the choice of technology.

Influence of Industry and Firm-Specific Characteristics

Although the empirical evidence so far has not allowed for a testing of the alternative explanations as to why technology choice has not led to full employment, it has pointed to significant differences in the characteristics of the technologies chosen among industries and—within an industry—between firms. Here it is commonly acknowledged that industry characteristics influence the profile of the technologies chosen. Difficulties encountered by previous studies in comparing technology choices in different industries, however, have resulted in little agreement over identifying these characteristics. Chemical industries are generally described as more capital intensive than mechanical industries. Yet it has not been shown whether this was due to differences in the spectrum of available alternatives or in the pattern of technology choice.

Important differences of behavior have also been found among firms in the same industry. Such differences include national origin (foreign versus local), ownership (public versus private), management profile, and strategy.[4] Although these patterns have been better researched than the differences between industries, the contradictory findings made for them lead to the questioning of some of the variables that have been considered relevant and of the rationale behind them. For example, since foreign firms have been found alternatively to adopt more capital-intensive and more labor-intensive technologies, the fact that they are foreign might not be the best explanatory variable of their technology choices.

Previous Studies

Four basic weaknesses can be found in most of the studies of technology choice in developing countries that have been conducted so far.[5] To a large extent, these shortcomings in methodology explain the often contradictory nature of their findings and the lack of acceptance of these findings as definitive.

At the outset most studies fail to identify and separate the main reasons that should lead to the choice of different technologies in different environments. They do not recognize differences in the scale of production, in the characteristics of the inputs or the output, and in factor prices. Secondly, practically all of these studies lack a frame of reference against which to evaluate the technology choice made by specific firms. This is because they do not first establish the range of alternatives available to the decision maker. Thirdly, the quantitative tool used to compare technologies and evaluate their suitability to a specific environment takes only two very aggregated factors—capital and labor—into consideration. Finally the tools used to assess technology choices do not allow for the identification and isolation of country-specific, industry-specific, and firm-specific factors that influence technology choice.

Differences in Factor Costs: Defining the Observational Units

In most other studies little emphasis is placed on isolating the impact of differences in scale of production, in input or output characteristics, and in the factor cost structure that firms must consider in choosing a technology. Since the focus of these studies is the adaptation of technology to factor prices, their authors tend to attribute all of the differences in production technologies encountered to differences in factor prices. But this tends to blur the results and make their interpretation difficult. It may also introduce a systematic bias into their results since production facilities in developing countries are generally of a smaller size than in developed ones.

To a large extent this weakness can be traced to the definition and selection of the observation units on which most of these studies are based. The choice of technology observation unit most often used is an entire, contiguous production facility.[6] The technologies used by these entire plants are compared, and alternative technology choices must then be defined at the plant level. In order to isolate differences in technology caused by differences in the cost of the factors of production, only plants of comparable scale of production, input, and output characteristics and age of equipment should be compared.

Such requirements are extremely difficult, if not impossible, to fulfill because: there is a lack of comparability between whole factory processes due to differences in the input and/or output mix; in any given industry and developing country, there are usually very few plants, let alone plants of identical size; and devising alternative technologies for an entire plant poses problems of line balancing.

In most cases it is impossible to determine the age of a plant since the equipment in it has been installed at different times. For each expansion of capacity or renovation, equipment is brought in to add to or replace older equipment. This causes a variation in age of equipment even in the same processing step.

Even if such a plant is entirely built and equipped on the same date, it normally is the product of a number of discrete investment decisions. The summation of all of these into some aggregate measure of technology appropriateness probably results in overlooking individual choices whose impact might have cancelled each other out and does not provide much insight into the process of analysis and choice followed by the decision makers.

The inquiry presented in this book showed that these investment decisions tend to coincide with processing steps. It is logical, therefore, to examine each processing step of a facility separately and to take note of the technology decision made for that processing step. Therefore such investment decision units instead of complete manufacturing processes were chosen as the basic observational unit of this study.

Although industry practice was followed as much as possible in defining investment decisions, an investment decision may be described as a group of machines purchased at the same time that are performing the same processing step in the overall production sequence. Thus if all machines used in a processing step were installed at the same time, they will constitute an investment decision. If because of equipment replacement or expansion of capacity, machines performing a processing step were purchased at different periods, each group of machines purchased at the same time will be considered as an investment decision.

A final problem in defining a unit of observation for this study is that in most production sequences, a processing step usually is performed not by a set of identical machines but by identical clusters of machines. In each such cluster there is normally a main piece of equipment and a set of auxiliary pieces of equipment, such as driving engines, pumps, and control devices. The choice, then, is either to collect information and identify alternatives for each piece of equipment of the cluster or to aggregate these pieces of equipment.

It is impractical to try to collect information on each of these pieces of equipment; for example, a pulp and paper mill is composed of some 10,000 such pieces of equipment, among which there are approximately 6,000 pumps and 3,000 engines to drive the processing equipment, while there are only a hundred or so pieces of equipment doing the actual processing. Also, given the broad practice of the industry in evaluating alternatives, it was decided to aggregate the auxiliary equipment with the main processing machine into an observational unit. Investment costs and input requirements, including labor, collected for this study will therefore refer to these clusters. Such a practice should lead to more reliable conclusions than considering only the main processing machine without taking the auxiliary equipment into account. This should allow for differences in the cost of the auxiliary equipment required by alternative technologies to be taken into account in making a choice between these alternatives.

To conclude, the use of observational units so defined has several advantages over the comparison of the technology of whole plants.

1. It corresponds more closely to the pattern of decision making in the firm.

2. It results in observational units that are more easily comparable since differences in the characteristics of inputs and/or output mix result in the addition, deletion, or increased emphasis on certain processing steps rather than important changes in the function of these steps.

3. It allows for a more precise definition of comparable scales of production for the purpose of technology choice in a given processing step, therefore making it possible to decide if two observational units are comparable regardless of the size of the plants in which they operate.

4. It makes it possible to give a precise age to a unit and to compare decisions that were made at roughly the same time, from among the same range of alternatives.

Creating a Frame of Reference: Defining the Alternatives

All previous studies have been based on comparisons of the technology used in a specific plant against the factor availability in the country in which this plant is located or on comparisons of the technologies adopted in different plants producing roughly similar goods and located in similar environments.

Several limitations exist when comparing a chosen technology to factor availability since the assumption is made that for the production of a given good, a technology combining the factors of production in a proportion equal to their availability must always exist. The existence of such a technology is in fact one of the basic issues in the choice of a technology and cannot be pushed aside by means of an assumption. When the technologies used by different plants are compared, the assumption is made that if enough plants are investigated, all of the available technologies will be used by at least one plant and therefore will be taken into consideration. This assumption runs to the core of the question to be answered: if all firms use the same technology, should the conclusion be that the choice-of-technology issue is a false one since there are no alternatives? Or is it a crucial one since alternatives are not chosen?

An alternative study design is to compare the technology choices made by firms to a systematic inventory of all of the alternatives available. Only by defining all of the alternative technologies available for the production of a given good can the optimum choice in a given environment be identified and the choices made by specific firms compared to this optimum. Such a procedure will provide insight into the reasons for adapting or not adapting to factor prices by application of such a procedure and the real costs, both financial and economic, of choices that depart from the optimum can be ascertained in this way.

In this inquiry the technology choices made by the firms studied will be evaluated by matching them up against an independently established spectrum of alternatives available at the time of the choice. In each of the two industries studied a systematic effort was made to identify the characteristics of all the models offered by equipment suppliers for each of the processing steps for which technology choices were analyzed. These models were then grouped into clusters according to their technical and operating characteristics. The clusters, or alternative technologies thus defined, constitute the whole range of alternatives from which the decision maker could choose. This technological range is not unlimited and continuous as assumed by neoclassical economic theory, but neither is it restricted to technologies already chosen by the firms studied.

Measuring Technology Appropriateness: Developing a Quantitative Yardstick

Capital-labor Ratios
Although there have been notable exceptions, most other studies of technology choice are based on the use of various ratios of capital to labor, capital to output, or labor to output for the purpose of comparing technologies and examining the technologies' appropriateness to a specific environment.[7]

The use of such ratios in the context of technology choice poses several important problems. These ratios are industry dependent and therefore do not allow for interindustry comparisons unless one assumes that different degrees of capital intensity between industries are only the result of different patterns of technology choice. They are likely to vary according to the size of production facilities in any industry in which there are economies of scale. They are dependent upon the level of capacity utilization attained by a firm. As a result, if care is not exercised in selecting observational units and in interpreting results, the analyst might obtain different values for these ratios among firms that use the same technology or have the same pattern of technology choice. In other situations similar values might actually conceal differences in technology or behavior.

These ratios, even in their most sophisticated form, also limit the study to the consideration of only two factors of production: labor and capital. They exclude from the comparisons other factors in the choice of a production technology such as raw material usage, power consumption, spare parts requirements, and processing chemicals usage. Furthermore they assume the homogeneity of the labor and capital factors of production. The labor factor of production, however, is an aggregation of supervisory, skilled, semiskilled, and unskilled workers whose cost and availability often vary widely within a developing country.[8] In the same way capital may be required either in the form of local currency or of foreign exchange whose relative availability might also vary. Finally it is impossible to evaluate the costs or benefits that may accrue to a country or a firm by choosing one technology rather than another from an analysis of these ratios.

For these reasons capital-labor ratios will not be used in this study to characterize alternative technologies or to evaluate technology choices. Instead alternative technologies will be defined by their production input structure. The relative suitability of these alternatives to a specific environment will then be evaluated in terms of the production costs that would result from applying the prevailing input and factor prices to the technologies' production input structures.

Production Input Structures
The production input structure of a technology may be defined as the quantity in physical terms of each input (capital in local currency and in foreign exchange, different skills of labor, raw materials, spare parts, utilities, and so forth) needed for the production of a given quantity of output through the use of that technology. Each technology can thus be identified by its production input structure and each environment by the cost of these different inputs. At a given scale of production, technology adaptation then becomes a matter of matching the input

structure of a technology with the factor price structure of a country in order to minimize production cost.

The use of production input structures to characterize differing technologies has an advantage over capital-labor ratios in that it does not limit the analysis to the consideration of only two factors of production. Differences in the rate of consumption of power, spare parts, raw materials, and other factors between two alternative technologies can be taken into account, thus resulting in a more realistic representation of the choices available to a country or a firm. They also allow for the consideration of differences between the skills required to operate alternative technologies. In the same manner they enable an investigation of differences in the cost of local currency and foreign exchange funds. This becomes important, for example, when equipment of one technology is available locally but equipment of another must be imported.

The production input structures of all alternative technologies were derived for each technology choice decision examined. Applying the factor cost structure of a country to the production input structure of a technology yielded the cost of production using this technology in that environment. If the market price (price to the firm) of the factors of production is used in this computation, the resulting production cost should be the actual cost to the manufacturer. If the economic price (shadow price) of the factors of production is used, the production cost should then be the economic cost to the country.

Based on such a representation of the spectrum of available alternative technologies this system of computation can generate quantitative estimates that answer some fundamental questions about technology choice. For example, it is possible to evaluate the impact of factor price distortions on technology choice and its economic cost. Quantitative estimates can also be made of the potential for adaptation when going from one country to another and the cost and benefits accruing to a firm and to its host country when it chooses one technology over another.

Comparing Technology Choices: Developing an Adaptation Index

To identify the considerations that influence technology choice, the choices made by firms with different characteristics need to be compared. Studies that employ capital-labor ratios to define technologies do not allow for meaningful interindustry comparisons. In fact even in the same industry they may yield unreliable results if such ratios are used to compare technology choices made in different production steps.

For example, a firm in industry A invested $10,000 in equipment per job created. At the same time a firm in industry B invested $30,000 per job created. Does that mean that the firm in industry A was more prone to choose labor-intensive technologies than the firm in industry B? If the spectrum of alternative technologies had been the same in industries A and B, the answer would be yes. But the answer would be different if the available alternative technologies in industry A were to range from $5,000 to $12,000 per job created, while in industry B, they ranged from $30,000 to $50,000. In that eventuality, the firm in industry B should be considered more prone to adopt labor-intensive alternatives than the firm in industry A. A similar example could be furnished to point to the dangers of using capital-labor ratios to compare the choices of technology made in different processing steps of the same industry.

Clearly an index of technology choice is needed that would be independent of the range of alternatives available to perform a specific operation. This would inform an investigator where the technology chosen is located in the range of alternatives. Comparing the values of this index in different processing steps, in firms of different characteristics, in different countries, and in different industries would then permit the identification of the factors influencing technology choice.

An index measuring the propensity of firms to adapt their technology choice to the cost of the factors of production they encounter was developed for this study. This index indicates the position of the technology chosen relative to the technology that would minimize production cost in that environment and the technology that minimizes production cost in the United States. (The technology that minimizes production cost in the United States was used as a reference point since it was considered to be representative of the technology choice made in a capital-rich, labor-poor economy.) This index is based on the production cost that each of these three technologies would have yielded in the economic context in which the plant were to be situated.

Methodology of the Study

In this study the technology choices made by twenty-eight firms in developing countries were investigated, using the parameters described. The analysis sequence outlined below was followed for each technology choice. This inquiry is based on a previously established list of alternative technologies available to perform the operation considered, as well as a definition of each of these alternatives in terms of its input structure. A notational description of this analysis sequence is shown in table 1.1.

Measurement of the Potential for Adaptation

The potential for adaptation is defined as the production cost savings that can be realized by using the technology optimum for the factor costs the plant must pay, as compared with the technology optimum for United States factor prices. In the quantitative analysis of these data, the following neoclassical definition of optimality has been adopted: In a given environment the optimal technology is defined as the one yielding the lowest production cost. The assumption here is that the decision maker's only objective in making a technology choice is to minimize production costs. Of course, other considerations might influence the technology choice decision. One of the aims of this study is to identify them.

The potential for adaptation in each technology choice studied is computed in the following manner:

1. The cost of the factors of production to the firm is applied to the production input structure of each of the alternative technologies. From this is computed the production cost that would result from the use of each of these alternatives.

2. The technology giving the lowest production cost is selected as the optimum technology for that firm.

3. The technology yielding the lowest production cost at U.S. factor prices is selected as the U.S. technology.

4. The production cost that would be incurred by the firm if it were to choose the U.S. technology is selected to be the production cost without any technology adaptation.

5. The potential for adaptation is equal to the difference between the production cost that would prevail if this firm were to use the U.S. technology and the production cost if it were to adopt the optimum technology for its factor costs.

This potential for adaptation is a measure of the production cost savings that the firm would realize if it employed the technology most

Table 1.1
Analysis of a Technology Choice Decision

Structure of Production Input	Inputs at Market Prices LDC A		Inputs at Shadow Prices LDC A	
U.S. Technology	X_{US} =	Private production cost without adaptation	Y_{US} =	Social production cost without adaptation
Technology used in LDC A	X_A =	Private production cost with present adaptation	Y_A =	Social production cost with present adaptation
Alternative Tech$_1$	X_1 =	Private production cost using Alt. Tech$_1$	Y_1 =	Social production cost using Alt. Tech.$_1$
Alternative Tech$_2$	X_2 =	Private production cost using Alt. Tech$_2$	Y_2 =	Social production cost using Alt. Tech.$_2$
Alternative Tech$_3$	X_3 =	Private production cost using Alt. Tech$_3$	Y_3 =	Social production cost using Alt. Tech.$_3$

Step 1
The technology having the smallest X, X_i, is the optimum technology from the private point of view (market prices) in LDC A.
The technology having the smallest Y, Y_j, is the optimum technology from the social point of view (shadow prices) in LDC A.
$X_{US} - X_i$ = Potential for adaptation at market prices in LDC A.
$Y_{US} - Y_j$ = Potential for adaptation at shadow prices in LDC A.

Step 2
$Y_i - Y_j$ = Economic cost of factor cost distortions in LDC A.

Step 3
$X_{US} - X_A$ = Private savings realized by present level of adaptation in LDC A.
$Y_{US} - Y_A$ = Economic value of present level of adaptation in LDC A.

Step 4
$$\frac{X_{US} - X_A}{X_{US} - X_i} = \text{Propensity to adapt exhibited in technology choice decision studied.}$$
$$= f \text{ (explanatory variables)}$$

closely suited to its cost of the factors of production instead of the technology best suited to U.S. conditions.

These computations will first be made using the cost to the firm, or market price, of the factors of production. When the market price of the factors is used, the optimum obtained is the one for the private decision maker. The potential for adaptation represents the savings this decision maker would then reap from full adaptation. These computations should then be repeated using the economic (or shadow) price of the factors. The economic cost of the factors leads to an optimum, which is based on the availability of these factors rather than on their possibly distorted market prices. The optimum, then, is the one for the country rather than for the private decision maker. The potential for adaptation becomes the measure of the economic savings, rather than monetary savings, to be made from full adaptation.

Measurement of the Economic Cost of Factor Price Distortions

Factor price distortions exist when the market prices of the factors of production do not fully reflect the relative availability of these factors and therefore their economic value. Such factor price distortions should cause the optimum technology—as determined on the basis of market costs—to be different from the optimum technology determined on the basis of economic costs. The private decision maker will then be pushed toward a choice of technology that may be cost minimizing from his or her point of view but might not be so from the country's point of view. Even if this manager were to behave according to the precepts of neoclassical economic theory and choose what he or she perceives to be the cost-minimizing technology, the host country might still suffer economic costs resulting from these distortions.

The additional economic costs resulting from factor price distortions can be quantified using the framework developed to measure the potential for adaptation. They are equal to the difference between the economic cost of production of the market optimum technology and the economic cost of production of the social optimum technology.

Evaluation of the Amount of Technology Adaptation that Took Place

Each of the technology choice decisions examined resulted in the adoption of one of the alternatives. The next step is to evaluate this choice in relation to the optimum technologies already identified and to the U.S. technology.

A measure of the amount of adaptation that took place is derived in the following way:

1. The cost of the factors to the firm, when applied to the production input structure of the technology the firm actually chose, gives the actual production cost of the firm, given its current level of technology adaptation.

2. The value of the amount of adaptation that took place is the difference between this production cost and the production cost that would result from the use of the U.S. technology in that facility.

The computations in this step are first done using the market price of the factors of production and then using the economic costs of these factors. The use of the market prices of the factors of production yields a measure of the amount of adaptation done, which is equal to the financial savings the firm realized by choosing the technology it selected rather than the U.S. technology. The use of the economic costs of the factors leads to an evaluation of the social cost of production of the chosen technology to the host country. The measure of the adaptation that has occurred then becomes the economic savings realized by the firm's choosing this technology rather than the U.S. technology.

Derivation of the Propensity to Adapt

The degree to which this measure of adaptation depends upon the range of alternatives available and the general level of production costs confines its usefulness to comparisons of technology choices within the same processing step. To make possible interstep and interindustry comparisons, a normalized measure of adaptation needs to be developed.

The propensity to adapt referred to here is defined as the ratio of the value, at market prices of the factors, of the adaptation done by a firm to the value (also at market prices of the factors) of the potential for adaptation. This measure of the propensity to adapt of a firm identifies where its technology choice is positioned between the U.S. technology and the optimum technology at market prices of the factors of production. Therefore it is independent of the range of alternative technologies available and of the level of production costs.

Values taken by the propensity to adapt for different technology choices can then be explained by country-related, industry/product-related, and firm-related variables. Such an analysis should lead to the identification and appraisal of the considerations that influenced technology choice.

The Firms Studied

The firms were chosen so as to allow enough variation in those variables that are considered to influence a choice-of-technology decision most heavily. The determinants of technology choice identified in previous studies can be classified into industry-related, country-related, and company-related variables.

Among the industry-related variables the number of alternative technologies available to perform a given operation, as well as the type and scope of the trade-off between factors of production that characterize these alternatives, could have an important bearing on the questions to be answered. For example, although few studies of the choice of technology in chemical processes exist in the literature, it appears that the type of transformation process (mechanical versus chemical) is a determinant of the propensity of a firm to adapt its technology. Some other industry-related variables that should be examined are the level of competition (also country related) and the cost of information.

The main country-related variable in this inquiry is the cost of the factors of production. The economic costs of the factors of production are clearly country related because they depend only upon the demand and supply of these factors within a country. Some of the market prices of factors are also country related, such as the exchange rate and the cost of power if it is produced outside the firm. Others, such as the cost of capital and the efficiency of the work force, are company-related variables. Still others, such as the cost of the different types of labor, are both country and company related since the company can decide to deviate from the country norm. Policy-related variables, such as tax rates and protection granted, and items such as the local portion of each technology's equipment cost are also country-related variables.

The characteristics of the firm are company-related variables. They include the ownership of the company, its decision process to choose a technology, its market positioning, and the size of its production facilities.

Based on this analysis of what are considered to be relevant variables, the following sample was selected.

Industries

Two industries were selected because they were thought to have widely different characteristics and would therefore yield interesting comparisons:

• Textile: The spinning and weaving of short staple fibers (cotton or artificial or mixes of the two) into gray cloth.

• Pulp and paper: The sulfate process pulping of wood, with or without bleaching and chemical recuperation, and papermaking.

In its spinning and weaving steps the textile industry is a mechanical process industry. An old industry in both developing and developed countries, its technology has evolved slowly and is widely available from equipment manufacturers. It is probably the most widespread industry in developing countries. As of 1974 50 percent of the looms and 48 percent of the spindles of the world were installed in developing countries.[9] It is also an industry in which large multinational corporations and foreign investment do not play an important role. U.S. multinational textile companies represented only 5.9 percent of the sales and 9.6 percent of the assets of all U.S. textile companies in 1966. This is compared against an average for all industries of 39.2 percent and 45.7 percent, respectively.[10] Subsidiaries of multinational companies produce a negligible amount of the textile output of developing countries.

The pulp and paper industry is a chemical process industry for the most part. In its advanced industrial form, it is a new industry for developing countries. Its technology has evolved rapidly, is highly sophisticated, is mastered by only a few large firms, equipment manufacturers, and consulting companies, and is highly proprietary. It is not a common industry in developing countries. Developing countries produce only 5 percent of the world's output of pulp and paper—an even lower percentage than their already low share of world consumption. Developed countries' firms play a major role in this industry although this role is understated by the figures about multinational pulp and paper companies. Multinational companies account for only 21.8 percent of the sales and 24 percent of the assets of U.S. pulp and paper companies.[11] These relatively low figures, however, are explained by the capacity of developed countries' firms in this industry to resist pressures to produce in developing countries. Although developing countries offer large wood resources and better growing conditions than do developed countries, the number of ventures in these countries by developed countries' firms has remained small. At the same time few local firms have been able to put together the technical knowledge and the management skills needed to start such large ventures.

In each of these two industries, manufacturing activities—spinning and weaving of short staple fiber in textile and sulfate pulping of wood and papermaking in pulp and paper—were selected on the basis of two criteria: that the plants undertaking these activities be comparable in terms of their input and output and that the same range of alternatives be available for all technology choices.

Countries

Colombia, Brazil, Indonesia, and the Philippines were selected as the developing countries where manufacturing facilities were to be examined. The reason for their selection was that these countries are at different stages of industrial development, although all of these countries are relatively large. Large countries were chosen because of the need to have several textile and pulp and paper plants available for study in each country.

Country size might introduce a bias that would appear when extrapolating from the results of this study, however. The existence of a large market means that foreign companies and foreign equipment suppliers will automatically exhibit more interest. The presence of several producing companies in one industry also leads to a higher degree of competition. As will be shown later, these factors would lead to overestimating the propensity of firms to adapt to the local cost of the factors of production.

Production Facilities

For each industry a minimum of two production facilities was selected in each country, with the exception of Japan and the United States. The exact number of facilities selected depended upon the number of plants that satisfied the selection criteria used. Only in Brazil was the number of plants large enough to make it impossible to study all those that qualified.

The production facilities whose technology choices were to be studied were selected with two criteria in mind. First, their scales of production were to be as close as possible to each other in order to facilitate the matching of scale at the production step level. Second, their facilities, or at least part of their facilities, needed to have been constructed after 1970 and in operation at the time of the data collection (June 1975–April 1976). Within these constraints the companies were to have characteristics as varied as possible, in particular with regard to their ownership.

Table 1.2 shows the exact size and composition of the sample of firms on which this study was conducted. To the extent possible, the data collected from the production facilities and equipment manufacturers were based on actual operating conditions. Data collection for the manufacturing facilities normally took one to two days and for the equipment manufacturers half a day to a day, depending on the range of equipment they manufactured.

Definition of Some Concepts

The terms *alternative technologies, choice of technology, adaptation,* and *appropriateness* have been used so far without being defined. Although these concepts are fundamental to the technology choice issue, some of the controversy surrounding this issue can be traced to the different interpretations these terms receive in various disciplines, particularly in engineering and economics.

There are two basic definitions of *technology*: the engineering and the economic. To the engineer a technology is a transformation process, a way of combining inputs to obtain an output with given characteristics. It is thus primarily defined in terms of the operations and equipment it requires. Economists, on the other hand, define technology in terms of the type and quantity of each input, including capital, required to produce a given quantity of output, rather than in terms of the transformation process that takes place. To economists what engineers call a technology becomes a "black box" defined by what goes in and what comes out.

These two definitions of technology do not exactly coincide. Engineers will consider two production processes to be the same technology— or at most different techniques of production—as long as the principles and methods used are basically the same. This is despite the fact that the input mixes might be different. For economists this difference in

Table 1.2
Composition and Size of the Sample

	United States and Canada	Europe	Japan	Colombia	Brazil	Philippines	Indonesia	Total
Producing companies								
Textile	1		2	3	2	5	6	19
Pulp and paper	2			2	5	3	2	14
Equipment manufacturers								
Textile	3	10	4	1				18
Pulp and paper		5			1			6
Engineering and consulting firms								
Textile		1						1
Pulp and paper	2	1						3
Professional organizations and government organization								
Industrial			1	2	3	2	2	10
Textile	1		1			1	1	4
Pulp and paper					1	1	1	3

input requirements will turn these two production processes into two distinct technologies.

Throughout this investigation the word *technology* is used in the economic sense. Minor changes in production techniques as well as fundamental process innovations are called *different technologies* if they result in differences in input requirements.

The concept of technology choice is based on the assumption that alternative technologies are available for the production of a given good. Again the engineering and the economic definitions of what should be considered alternative technologies differ widely. Such a divergence is attributable to the definition given by each discipline of what is to be construed as the same product.

For engineers a product is defined by a number of precise technical characteristics. A sheet of paper is defined by as many as twenty characteristics, measuring aspects as varied as its weight per unit of surface, its brightness, its smoothness, its resistance to burst and to tear, and its degree of absorption of water. A piece of cloth is characterized in the same way by some thirty variables, ranging from the characteristics of the yarn used in making the cloth to the types and number of imperfections in the cloth. Because of this degree of precision in the engineering definition of a product, practically no two processes or types of equipment can produce the same product. Therefore engineers will argue that once the product is defined, the number of alternative technologies available to produce it is very small, if there are any such alternatives at all.

In economic terms a product is defined by the need it fills and the market it is designed to reach. For economists the output of two different technologies becomes the same product if the market considers them as readily substitutable. Packaging papers that have a different resistance to burst and tear will be considered as different products in the economic sense, while slight variations in their color will not make them different products to an economist. Industrial backing cloth of different strengths or different shades of color will be considered as different products by engineers, but only different strengths will make them different products for the economist since different shades of color do not influence its end use.

In this study the decision to consider various technologies as alternatives for the production of a product is based on the economic definition of that product. No in-depth study, however, could be made of the substitutability of goods of different technical characteristics in each of the markets served by the firms studied. Therefore the amount of arbitrary judgment involved in deciding what should be considered as alternative technologies was minimized by allowing only limited variations in the characteristics of the end product. Conceivably paper of the newsprint type, produced by a mechanical pulping process, could be sold as writing paper in Indonesia, given the lower quality requirements of that market. It would therefore be a substitute for the bleached caustic soda paper currently used, and these two technologies should be considered as alternative technologies. Since only an in-depth technical and market study could answer this question, however, the two technologies were not considered as alternatives in this study. Such restrictive behavior would result in an underestimation by this study of the range of alternative technologies available.

A choice between alternative technologies has to be made according to one or several criteria. An infinite number of criteria can be used to compare technologies and choose among them. One might want to select the newest technology or the technology that requires equipment that has the smallest number of moving parts. According to economic theory, however, the criterion to be used for a choice between alternative technologies should be the minimization of production cost. The use of this criterion in comparing alternative technologies leads to two concepts used throughout this study and that should therefore be defined: the concept of efficiency and that of adaptation or appropriateness.

On the basis of production cost minimization, a technology is considered as more efficient than another if it should always be chosen over the other, whatever the availability and price of the different factors of production. Such a situation will occur only if to produce a given quantity of a good, a technology uses less of some factors of production and an equal amount of the remaining factors as compared to another technology.

In most cases, however, alternative technologies combine the factors of production in such a way that each requires more of some factors of production but less of others than its alternatives. In such cases, one technology cannot be considered more efficient than its alternatives since their relative attractiveness will depend upon the cost of the various factors of production. It will then be decided that a technology is more adapted to a specific environment than another if it results in a lower cost of production given factor costs in that environment.

Because of some of its uses, the word *adapted* has gathered an ethnocentric connotation, implying that the technology suited to local conditions is the result of a transformation of the developed countries' technology. In this study the word *adapted* is used as meaning "suited" and therefore is interchangeable with the word *appropriate*.

2   The Scope for Adaptation

Are alternative technologies available for the production of a given good at industrial scale? If the answer to this question is positive, a second equally important question follows: Do the available alternative technologies make use of the factors of production in proportions different enough for the choice between them to have a significant impact on the demand for these factors?

In the textile and pulp and paper industries a significant number of alternative technologies exists for most processing steps.[1] This finding is all the more meaningful since a rather restrictive definition of what technologies may be considered as alternatives was adopted, and only technologies embodied in equipment currently available from equipment manufacturers were considered. The nature of these alternatives differs significantly between a mechanical process industry such as textile and a chemical process industry such as pulp and paper. In the former alternative technologies are incorporated into the main production machinery. But in chemical process industries alternative technologies take the form of options in the choice of control mechanisms for the main piece of equipment. To a large extent the difference in the nature of alternative technologies that are available within these two types of industries explains the conflicting results of previous studies.

The range of usage of the different factors of production embodied in the alternative technologies that were identified is wide enough to make the choice of technology a highly relevant macroeconomic variable. For example, the most labor-intensive alternative requires between three and fifteen times the amount of labor input of the most capital-intensive one. Even more important differences in the composition of the labor force and in the form of capital required by these alternative technologies make focusing on the technology choice issue even more imperative.

Before turning to the identification and analysis of the alternative technologies available in the textile and pulp and paper industries, a brief description of the production processes in the two is in order.

The Textile Production Process: Short Fiber Spinning and Weaving

A short fiber spinning and weaving mill is divided into four sections: the opening room, the spinning shed, the preparatory section, and the weaving shed. To these could be added a finishing department, but this step has not been included in this study because of the difficulty in finding comparable finishing facilities. This problem results from the great variety of processes in use by the industry.[2] (See the production process diagram of a short fiber spinning and weaving mill in figure 2.1. A more detailed description of the various processing steps is found in appendix B.)[3]

Preliminary Steps: The Blow Room

Three processing functions are performed in the opening room: plucking (also called breaking or opening), cleaning, and scutching (also called picking). The aim of these operations is to mix the fibers from different bales, to break up the clods of compressed cotton from the bales, and to clean the cotton of foreign matter that has not been separated during the ginning process. Since efficient spinning and weaving is only possible from a very uniform fiber mix, the blending of cottons from different bales is necessary in order to eliminate the small variations among bales in the physical characteristics of raw cotton. These three steps are performed in a continuous manner as the cotton is conveyed from one machine to another by moving belt or by air flow through ducts.

Spinning

The spinning shed usually houses five processing steps: carding, drawing, roving, spinning and winding. To obtain a very high-quality yarn, a sixth processing step, combing, which consists of removing the shorter fibers, can be incorporated between the runs of the stock through the drawing frames. This step is not needed for yarn of ordinary quality.

After a final cleaning and a first disentanglement of the fibers at the carding step, the stock is run through drawing frames several times to

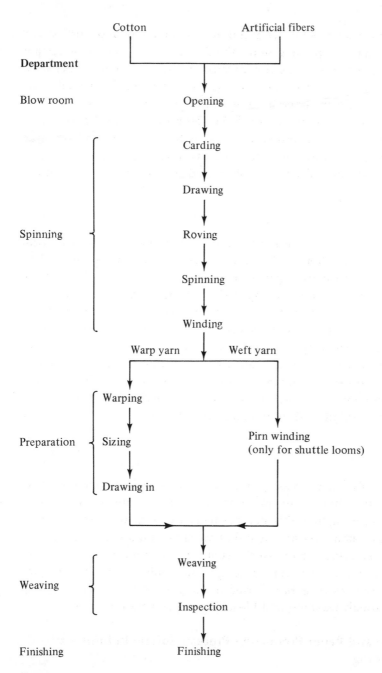

Figure 2.1
Steps in the Textile Manufacturing Process

disentangle the fibers further and draw them parallel into a fine sliver. In the roving and spinning steps, the thickness of this sliver is further reduced through the application of tension, and its strength is increased by means of twisting. In the winding step, the yarn is cleaned of irregularities and transferred from the small spinning bobbins onto larger packages. The fibers that entered the spinning shed in the form of a clean, opened, and unstructured mass will leave it wound on large bobbins (called cheeses or cones). This yarn can be used for weaving, knitting, or sewing and is commonly traded between firms and countries.

Preparation

The yarn enters the preparatory section in the form of large cylindrical or cone-shaped bobbins. They arrive directly from the spinning shed or from a yarn finishing department where the yarn was dyed or treated. The preparatory section is composed of a warp yarn section and a weft yarn section. The warp (thread that runs lengthwise) will constitute the base of the cloth. The weft yarn will be inserted across the warp threads at the weaving step. In the warp yarn section, a large number of threads is wound on a beam (warping) and dipped in starch to increase its resistance (sizing). In the weft yarn section, the thread is wound on bobbins adapted to the insertion mechanism of the looms used (pirn winding if shuttle looms are used).

Weaving

Although only one processing step, weaving, is performed in the weaving shed, the shed is an important part of the mill. In a balanced spinning-weaving mill, this step normally accounts for about one-third of the total capital investment and of the labor employed. The weaving shed's output is gray cloth, which usually goes to a finishing department after inspection for defects. Although commonly traded among firms and countries, cloth is rarely used in its gray form. At the very least it goes through washing and bleaching stages before final use.

The Pulp and Paper Production Process: Sulfate Pulping and Papermaking

A wide variety of processes can be used to produce paper pulp from wood. These processes are usually classified into three main categories:

mechanical, semimechanical, and chemical.[4] The choice among these main types of pulping processes is normally based on the characteristics of the required end product—that is, the kind of paper or cardboard that corresponds to the needs of the user. The sulfate or kraft pulping process is one of the existing chemical processes. Because of technical considerations and cost advantages, it has become the most commonly used chemical process. In fact most new facilities that employ a chemical pulping process now use the kraft process. Since only the sulfate process was considered in this study, the general industry name of pulp and paper will be used to refer to this process exclusively. (See figure 2.2)

A pulp and paper mill has four main departments: the wood yard, the pulp mill, the stock preparation department, and the paper mill. Through these four departments, the logs delivered to the wood yard are transformed into large reels of paper.

Three other departments can be added: the chemical recovery department, the bleaching department, and the finishing department. The bleaching and finishing departments were excluded from the scope of this study because of the wide variety of available processes. Another reason is that this choice will be dictated solely by market requirements in terms of the degree of whiteness and format of the paper required. The chemical recovery department was also excluded because the complexity of the process and the changes it undergoes depending upon the availability and cost of various chemicals make it difficult to find comparable facilities. (A more detailed description of the processing steps is found in Appendix B.)

Wood Yard

Wood is shipped from the forestry operations to the wood yard in the form of logs of varying size and length. The first operation performed in this wood yard is debarking by means of a mechanical process. These logs then go through a chipper where they are cut into pieces small enough to allow for chemical treatment.

Since the wood yard makes the link between the forestry operations, which work only during the daytime and are highly dependent upon the weather, and the pulp mill, which operates continuously, a chip storage step is normally added.

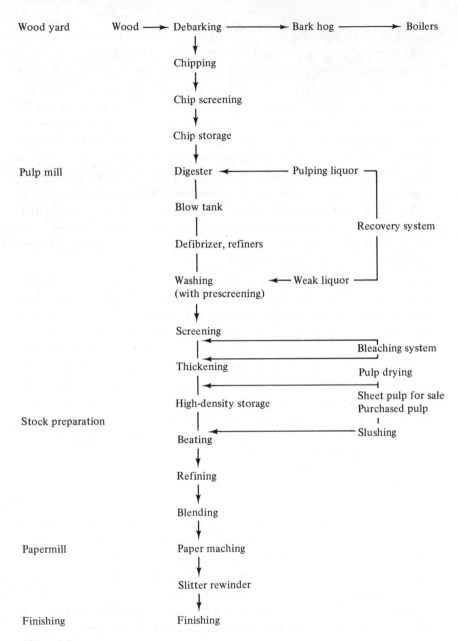

Figure 2.2
Steps in Sulfate Process Pulp and Paper Manufacturing

Pulp Mill

In the pulp mill the cellulose fibers from which paper is made are separated through chemical action from the lignin that binds them together in the wood. The lignin and chemicals are then removed, leaving a slurry of water and cellulose fibers. This is accomplished in a sequence of operations that starts with the digesting step. Here the lignin is dissolved through the combined action of heat, pressure, and chemicals without altering the structure of the cellulose fibers. Then comes a series of operations—blow tank, defiberizers, and refiners steps—where the cellulose fibers are disentangled and separated, first through a rapid drop in pressure and then through mechanical action. In the washing step that follows, the fibers are repeatedly washed to remove the lignin and the processing chemicals. After a screening step, which removes all the lumps of fibers that have not been separated, the stock is finally thickened and stored, ready for use by the stock preparation department or for drying and sale outside the mill.

Stock Preparation

Papermaking requires a very uniform stock, normally made up of different pulps of specific characteristics and of various additives. The stock will be ready for the paper machine when it leaves the stock preparation department. In this department all pulp is first reduced to a uniform consistency by a slushing operation. A beating step then prepares the fibers for easy bonding at the papermaking stage. Remaining lumps are eliminated in a screening operation before the stock proceeds to the blending stage where the different types of pulp are mixed together with the additives required to produce a specific type of paper.

Paper Mill

All of the paper mill operations are basically performed by only one type of machine, the paper machine, of which there are one or a very few working in parallel in each mill. The role of the paper machine is to remove progressively the water from the slurry admitted at one end of the machine in order to have the fibers assembled in a dry sheet of paper by the other end of the machine. The water is removed through the successive actions of gravity, suction, pressure, and heat.

Origin of the Data on Alternative Technologies

Information about the alternative technologies available to perform each production step in the two industries studied and input requirements including original investment cost of each of these technologies could be collected in either of two ways. It could originate from the textile and pulp and paper firms in the study, or it might be obtained directly from equipment manufacturers and engineering firms.

Collecting such data from the technology users introduces several important limitations. There is, for example, no guarantee that the firms surveyed will have identified all alternative technologies. If there is a low degree of technology adaptation and a limited part of the range of alternatives is used, it would be erroneous to assume that few alternative technologies are actually available in the industry. This limitation seems to have affected the results of a number of previous studies of technology choice.

Furthermore the information collected from the users presents serious problems of comparability. The countries in which production facilities were studied suffer from high inflation rates as a rule and frequently devalue their currencies. The equipment costs that may be encountered would therefore be highly influenced by the currency of payment, the date of order and delivery, the escalation clauses included in the contract, and the mode of payment. In this investigation, for example, no two facilities were started up on exactly the same date. In addition the equipment prices obtained from the users include all of the rebates and discounts negotiated. These rebates and discounts vary from purchaser to purchaser depending on the size of the order and the bargaining power of the firm, although it appears that the same rate of discount can be obtained by the same client from all equipment manufacturers. In the same way manning tables of different firms are not directly comparable because of differences in job definitions and job assignments. Therefore serious distortions in comparing technologies would be introduced if equipment data for each technology were to originate from different users.

Collecting data about alternative technologies directly from the equipment manufacturers circumvents many of these problems. First, their cost quotations are more precise and can be related to a specific date. Second, prices quoted by equipment manufacturers have the advantage of excluding any special package prices or rebates given to certain individual customers. This allows for comparisons of alternative technologies among manufacturers, but may lead to a slight over-estimation of equipment cost and thus an underestimation of the propensity of firms to adapt. Since all equipment cost data were collected in 1975–1976 and the plants studied were all built in the early 1970s it is reasonable to assume that no major changes in the relative cost of alternative technologies took place within the time span covered.

For the same reasons, manning tables of the alternative technologies and input requirements were also based on the equipment manufacturers' estimates. When used for a specific production facility, they were corrected for the level of labor efficiency that the firm attained.

Prices and input requirements were obtained for each type of machinery produced by all major textile and pulp and paper equipment manufacturers in the United States, Japan, and Europe. Those relatively rare equipment manufacturers in the developing countries in which the production facilities studied were located were also investigated. Data on the textile equipment manufacturers of India and Korea, the only two developing countries with substantial industries of this type, were obtained from secondary sources, mainly the World Bank. For the pulp and paper industry, whose equipment is often custom made, engineering firms specializing in such custom designs were an important source of data.

The alternative technologies described in the next section are all incorporated in equipment currently available from equipment manufacturers. Excluded from the spectrum of alternatives are past technologies that are no longer embodied in any manufactured equipment, as well as technically feasible technologies that require further research and development before commercialization. The alternatives presented are therefore realistic choices available to firms planning a new manufacturing facility.

The managers of the companies studied confirmed that the cost of equipment as well as the labor and other input requirements obtained for the investigation were realistic.

Alternative Technologies in Textile Production

A wide range of alternative technologies was found in this industry, although the number of alternatives varies greatly across steps.

For each step in the spinning and weaving process, the alternative technologies available are shown in table 2.1, in ascending order of mechanization and technological sophistication.[5] (A more detailed de-

Table 2.1
Alternative Technologies in the Textile Industry

Processing Steps	Number of Alternatives	Features	Alternative 1	Alternative 2	Alternative 3	Alternative 4
Plucking	3		Manual	Auto belt type	Auto carousel type	
Scutching	5	Output form	Lap	Lap	Lap	Lap
		Stoppage	Manual	Auto	Auto	Auto
		Doffing of lap	Manual	Auto	Auto	Auto
		Change of axis, weighting, coding, and storage	Manual	Manual	Auto	Auto
		Transfer to cards	Manual	Manual	Manual	Auto conveyor
Carding	7	Speed	Low speed[a]	Medium speed[b]	Medium speed[b]	High speed[c]
		Enclosure	No enclosure	Enclosure	Enclosure	Enclosure
		Waste collection	Manual	Pneumatic	Pneumatic	Pneumatic
				At machine level		
		Size of cans	Small cans	Small cans	Large cans, power coiling	Large cans, power coiling
		Doffing of cans	Manual	Manual	Manual	Manual
Drawing	4	Speed	Low speed[d]	High speed[e]	High speed[c]	Super high speed[f]
		Feeding	Cans	Cans	Cans	Ribbon fed
		Doffing of cans	Manual doffing	Manual doffing	Auto doffing	Auto doffing
		Number of deliveries	2 deliveries	2 deliveries	2 deliveries	1 delivery
Combing	4	Waste collection	Roll waste collection	Pneumatic waste collection	Pneumatic waste collection	Pneumatic waste collection
		Doffing and transfer of rolls	Manual	Manual	Auto doffing, manual transfer	Auto doffing, auto transfer
Roving	3	Doffing of spindles	Manual doffing	Easy doffing	Open end	

Alternative 5	Alternative 6	Alternative 7	Alternative 8	Alternative 9	Alternative 10	Alternative 11
Chute feeding of cards						
High speed[c]	High speed[c]	High speed[c]				
Enclosure	Enclosure	Enclosure				
Pneumatic	Pneumatic	Pneumatic				
	Centralized					
Large cans, power coiling	Large cans, power coiling	Automatic ribbon transfer				
Auto	Auto					

Table 2.1 (continued)

Processing Steps	Number of Alternatives	Features	Alternative 1	Alternative 2	Alternative 3	Alternative 4
Spinning	5	Piecing	Manual	Manual	Manual	Auto
		Doffing	Manual	Easy doffing	Traveling auto doffer	Stationary auto doffer
Winding	9	Feeding of spindles	Manual	Auto from 1 reserve position	Auto from rotary magazine	Auto from rotary magazine
		Doffing of spindles	Manual	Auto	Auto	Auto
		Feeding of cheese	Manual	Manual	Manual	Auto
		Doffing of cheese	Manual	Manual	Manual	Auto
		Knotting	Manual	Auto	Auto	Auto
Warping	2		Normal	Sectional		
Sizing						
Pirn winding	4	Feeding of pirns	Manual	Automatic from post magazine	Fully automatic	Unifil
		Doffing of pirns	Manual	Automatic manual collection	Automatic manual collection	Unifil
Weaving	11	Source of power	Hand loom	Power loom	Power loom	Power loom
		Transfer mechanism	Shuttle	Shuttle	Shuttle	Shuttle
		Change of filling	Nonauto	Nonauto	Shuttle change	Cop change
		Control of movement	Manual	Mechanical	Mechanical	Mechanical
		Other features				Less sophisticated version than tech 5 and 6

a. 5–10 kg/hr.
b. 15–20 kg/hr.
c. 20–30 kg/hr.
d. 150–300 m/mn.
e. 300–400 m/mn.
f. 500 m/mn.

Alternative 5	Alternative 6	Alternative 7	Alternative 8	Alternative 9	Alternative 10	Alternative 11
Open End						
Auto from rotary magazine plus prep station	Auto from rotary magazine plus prep station	Auto from bulk bin	Auto from bulk bin	Auto from auto transfer		
Auto	Auto	Auto	Auto	Auto		
Manual	Auto	Manual	Auto	Auto		
Manual	Auto	Manual	Auto	Auto		
Auto	Auto	Auto	Auto	Auto		
Power loom	Power loom	Power loom	Power loom	Power loom	Power loom	Power loom
Shuttle	Shuttle	Rigid rapier	Flexible rapier	Projective	Air jet	Multiphase
Cop change	Cop change	No need	No need	No need	No need	No need
Mechanical	Electronic	Electronic	Electronic	Electronic	Electronic	Electronic

scription of these alternatives is included in appendix B.) Some processing steps, however, will be excluded from the foregoing analysis, for the following reasons.

Combing: This processing step is only used in the manufacture of very fine yarns. Thus only a small number of the developing countries' production facilities included a combing step.

Roving and spinning: The technical complexity of the analysis for these steps led to their exclusion. This complexity stems from the fact that the only significant technological alternative—open-end spinning—substitutes for both steps and its economic viability depends upon the thickness of the yarn to be produced.

Warping and sizing: The study of these two steps was abandoned due to the lack of technological alternatives.

Alternative Technologies in Pulp and Paper Production

The alternative technologies available to the pulp and paper industry are shown in table 2.2. These technologies are arranged in ascending order of technological sophistication, which in effect means recency of discovery rather than degree of automation. For reasons that will be investigated below these alternatives are difficult to rank according to automation or factor usage. An examination of this technology alternatives table yields a few important conclusions.

Few technological alternatives exist for the major components in pulp and paper processing equipment. Except in the wood yard processing steps the existing alternatives seem to represent different technical ways in which a machine may perform the same function rather than different combinations of machine and labor. No specific form of measurement and control mechanism is assumed in the definition of these main pieces of equipment. For example, the operations of a technologically simple batch digester can be completely automated, while the operations of a sophisticated continuous digester can be manually controlled without changing the definition of these two technologies.

This characteristic requires elaboration since it has a major effect on the type of technology choices made in the pulp and paper industry. It contrasts with technology definition in the textile industry where one may easily evaluate the distribution of work between the machine and the operator. For example, a hand loom is defined as a loom in which all operations—throwing the shuttle, tacking, changing the frame's positions, and refilling the shuttle—are performed manually.

Table 2.2
Alternative Technologies in the Pulp and Paper Industry, Kraft Process

Step in Process	Number of Alternatives	Alternative 1	Alternative 2	Alternative 3
Wood handling	2	Manual	Cranes	
Debarking	2	Manual	Debarking drum	
Chip handling	3	Manual loading	Suction loading	Turntable loading
Digesting	3	Batch	Continuous Bauer	Continuous Kamyr
Refiners	3	Conical	Wide angle	Disc double disc
Washing	1	Drum washers		
Screening	3	Vibratory	Pressure	Centrifugal
Thickening	1			
Beating	4	Same as refining		
Paper machine				
Head box	1			
Sheet forming	3	Fourdrinier	Verti-Former	Ultra-Former
Press section	1			
Drying section	1			
Calender section	1			
Winding section	1			
Slitter rewinder	1			

Conversely the power shuttle change loom is defined as a loom that performs all of these functions automatically, by machine power. The operator merely prepares the shuttles and introduces them into the machine. The same categorization in terms of the distribution of work between labor and machine can be made when comparing a hand plucking system and a belt-type automatic plucking system.

In the pulp and paper industry, however, when looking into alternative technologies for major processing equipment, it is the way in which the machine's work is performed that becomes the critical definition factor. In the digesting step, for example, the cooking of the wood chips can be performed in batches or continuously. Furthermore, a Bauer continuous digester may be distinguished from a Kamyr continuous digester by the way in which the chips move from intake to discharge. All pulp refiners process the fibers by means of friction between two surfaces. The alternative technologies of pulp refiners differ in the shape and texture of these two surfaces: there is a Jordan conical refiner, a wide-angle refiner, and a disc refiner. These technological variations, however, have no direct effect on the number of workers required and their duties. These different technologies can be equipped so that their loading and unloading, as well as the flow of all inputs, may be manually controlled or, alternatively, computer controlled. It is this decision as to the mode of control of the processing machines, rather than the choice of technology of the processing equipment itself, that will have implications in terms of capital-labor trade-off.

Since such differences have an important impact on technology choice, a categorization of the ways in which alternative technologies offer trade-offs between the use of labor and capital is essential.

Technological Forms of Capital-Labor Trade-Offs

Differences between alternative technologies that result in capital-labor trade-offs can be classified into four main types: the degree of mechanization of a processing task, the degree of mechanization of a handling task, the degree of automation controls, and the unit's processing capacity.

Differences in Degree of Mechanization of a Processing Task

The mechanization of a processing task is the performance by a machine, rather than by a person, of an operation that affects the physical characteristics of a raw material. Examples are the introduction of automatic knotting into the winding step and the introduction of automatic mixing of the bales in the plucking step. Examples of alternative technologies whose differences fall into this category can easily be found in mechanical industries where the raw material is transformed through mechanical action. They can rarely be found in chemical industries where the raw material is transformed through chemical action for which there is no manual alternative.

Differences in Degree of Mechanization of a Handling Task

These may involve the mechanization of the loading and unloading of a machine or the mechanization of the transfer of an intermediate product from one processing step to another. Automatic pirn feeding and doffing and automatic package (cheese or cone) feeding and doffing in the winding step fall into this category, as do chute feeding of the cards in the scutching step and automatic ribbon transfer in the carding step. There is no theoretical reason why technological alternatives that do—or do not—include this category of mechanization should not be found in both mechanical and chemical industries. One could imagine a digester in the pulp and paper industry being loaded manually with wood chips and the digested pulp being transferred to the next processing step in wheelbarrows, as was in fact done a century ago. The high corrosiveness of the chemicals used and the high temperature of the reaction, however, would make manual handling too hazardous by today's standards. Furthermore the volumes of production of major pulp processing equipment that are dictated by economies of scale make this option impractical and uneconomical. An excessive amount of downtime would be required for manual loading and unloading of raw materials or intermediate products. A choice between alternative degrees of mechanization of handling tasks is therefore found mostly in mechanical processes, while chemical processes incorporate fully mechanized handling of raw materials and intermediate products.

Differences in Degree of Automation of Controls

Although there is much more choice as to the degree of mechanization of processing and handling operations in mechanical processes than in chemical ones, the chemical processes offer a wider range of opportunities for automation of control functions.

In a mechanical process a raw material is transformed through the application of physical actions. The number of processing variables is therefore limited, and production routines are relatively simple. Consequently the control function is neither complex nor expensive, therefore yielding no important technological choices. In a chemical process the number of inputs to be modified is generally larger. The number of variables to be controlled in the reaction is also much more important; they include temperature, pressure, flow of each of the chemicals, and time of the reaction. The control function is therefore more crucial than in mechanical processes and represents a larger portion of the investment decision. While the main equipment of chemical processes essentially consists of tanks in which reactions occur, plus piping to link them, offering few technological alternatives with capital-labor trade-off implications, chemical processing control equipment offers a wide range of alternatives encompassing a wider spectrum of human intervention levels.

A categorization of the alternative technologies available for the control of a variable, be it temperature, pressure, or flow, is presented in table 2.3. Among the several features defining the way in which a control function is performed, three were identified as having implications for employment: the location of the control mechanism, the driving force to adjust the controlled element, and the control source. Other considerations, such as whether transmission was electrical or by air pressure or whether the variable was recorded, were not considered meaningful for the purpose of this study. It appears that the potential for technology adaptation through changes in the control mode of chemical processes has been overlooked in most previous studies of chemical industries. As a result it has so far been considered that such industries exhibit a high degree of technological fixity or, in other words, do not offer opportunities for capital-labor trade-offs.

Differences in Unit Processing Capacities

At a given production level and with a given technology, the number of processing units used is generally not deemed to have labor usage implications. Where there is no change in technology, labor usage is considered to be proportional to total output rather than to the number of processing units used to produce that output. There are two exceptions to this rule, however. The first occurs when the control function occupies a large portion of the work force. The labor requirement of the control function of a piece of equipment—if no changes are made in its degree of mechanization or automation—will be the same whatever the capacity of this piece of equipment. In chemical manufacturing processes, where most of the direct labor is needed for control purposes, increases in a production unit's capacity will therefore result in substantial reductions in labor requirement per unit of output.

The second exception occurs when increases in machine capacity result from improvements in machine precision that permit higher speeds of operation. This situation is mostly found in mechanical processes. When this happens the maximum speed at which a machine can work is set by the precision of its operations, and a large proportion of the workers' time is spent intervening to correct mistakes resulting from machine imprecisions. In such cases an improvement in machine

Table 2.3
Proposed Categorization of Alternative Technologies for the Control Function of Chemical Processes

	Alternative 1	Alternative 2	Alternative 3	Alternative 4	Alternative 5	Alternative 6	Alternative 7
Location of control mechanism	At location of adjustment mechanism	At location of adjustment mechanism	At machine instrument panel	At machine instrument panel	At processing step instrument panel	At section instrument panel	At section instrument panel
Driving force of adjustment mechanism	Manual	Power	Power	Power	Power	Power	Power
Control source	Human	Human	Human	Automatic values set manually	Automatic values set manually	Automatic values set manually	Automatic values set automatically
Digesting Step: Variable Controlled							
Pressure			X				✓
Temperature			X				✓
Flow of wood chips	X						✓
Flow of pulping liquor		X					✓
Flow of steam		X					✓
Cycle of reaction			X				✓

X = labor-intensive alternative.
✓ = capital-intensive alternative.

precision allows higher speeds with an unchanged number of mistakes per unit of time and therefore unchanged labor requirements per machine. An example of this in the textile industry are the electronic controls on automatic cop-change looms. These controls allow higher weaving speeds without increasing the number of yarn breakages per hour, a result of improved precision in the movement of the shuttle. Since it is the weaver's duty to repair these yarn breakages and then to restart the loom when they occur, a weaver will be able to handle the same number of mechanical and electronically controlled automatic cop-change looms. Therefore less worker time will be required per unit of output on looms equipped with electronic controls.

Other Variables that May Affect Capital-Labor Trade-Offs

The choice between technological alternatives that result in a trade-off between labor and other inputs has been separated from the choice among technological alternatives that result in trade-offs between (two) inputs other than labor. In actual practice, nevertheless, there are cases where such a distinction is difficult to make. While the most important dimension of a choice might be the trade-off between two or more inputs other than labor, such a choice might still have certain labor usage implications. Cases such as this are found mostly in chemical processes in which the number of inputs is large and the relative importance of labor in the cost of production is small. One such example in the pulp and paper industry is the choice between batch and continuous digesters. Batch digesters are less expensive in terms of investment cost, but continuous digesters allow operating savings in steam, power, and some chemicals. Continuous digesters also happen to be larger than batch digesters. Typically one continuous digester is equivalent in production capacity to several batch digesters. Consequently even if the same control technology is used for both types, continuous digesters will require less labor for the same quantity of output. In such cases, the valuation of the main trade-offs tends to overshadow the impact of the choice on labor requirements.

Although the textile industry has so far been characterized as a mechanical process and the pulp and paper industry as a chemical process, this characterization is not entirely exact. In the textile industry, the sizing and finishing steps fall in the category of chemical processes, and in the pulp and paper industry, the wood yard operations and the finishing department should be considered mechanical processes. In fact an analysis of the alternative technologies in these particular steps confirms that they differ in the ways that have been associated with chemical and mechanical processes respectively.

The Range of Factor Usage in Alternative Technologies

With the knowledge that alternative technologies exist for most of the processing steps in the textile as well as the pulp and paper industries, it is important to determine whether these alternatives offer a sufficiently broad range of usage of the factors of production to make the choice-of-technology issue meaningful.

Factor Usage in the Textile Industry

In the textile industry, a precise quantification of the input requirement of the alternative technologies was possible. The range of factor usage they incorporate is summarized in table 2.4. An index value of 1.0 is assigned to the technology using the least amount of a given factor of production in a processing step. Each line gives the index value of the technology that uses the largest amount of that factor for each production step. The data contained in this table lead to some important conclusions.

The range of factor usage of the alternative technologies in the textile industry is large. The most labor-intensive technologies use up to fifteen times more labor than the least labor intensive (in three of seven processing steps, more than ten times). The most capital-intensive technologies consume between 150 percent and 400 percent of the capital requirement of the least capital-intensive ones (for this computation, the lowest construction cost found in our study was used to value buildings).

The range of labor usage is much larger than the range of capital usage. While the most capital-intensive technology called for only between 7 and 30 percent of the labor required by the most labor-intensive technology, the most labor-intensive technology still consumes between 25 and 60 percent of the amount of capital required by the most capital-intensive technology. This greater potential for savings on labor costs rather than on capital among alternative technologies can be attributed to the emphasis on labor savings that has governed technological innovation in the developed countries.

The technologies using the most labor do so mainly at the semiskilled/ operator level. In five of seven processing steps, the most labor-intensive

Table 2.4
Comparison of the Factor Requirements of the Technologies Using the Most and the Least of Each Factor in Each Production Step of the Textile Industry

Factor Requirements	Processing Steps						
	Plucking	Scutching	Carding	Drawing	Winding	Pirn Winding	Weaving[a]
Total labor requirements	3.1	11.5	14.3	2.2	8.2	4.5	11.5
Supervisory	1.9	3.3	5.7	1.6	3.4	2.3	3.2
Skilled	2.0	1.3	2.4	1.4	1.7	1.5	3.7
Semiskilled	9.9	b	29.9	4.7	18.0	5.4	19.1
Unskilled	2.0	19.0	23.7	2.0	1.0	1.0	2.5
Total investment requirements	1.6	1.8	1.8	1.5	3.4	2.9	3.9
Equipment	1.9	2.0	2.0	1.7	3.7	3.3	6.5
Buildings	1.0	1.4	1.5	2.7	1.5	b	1.3
Number of alternative technologies available	3	5	7	4	9	4	10

Note: 1.0 is the quantity of factor used by technology employing least amount of that factor. For each processing step an index value of 1.0 is given to the factor requirement of the alternative technology that uses the least amount of this factor. The value in each cell is the index value of the requirement of the factor of the technology that uses the largest amount of this factor.

a. Hand looms have not been included in this comparison since their choice would necessitate a completely different type of industrial organization beyond the scope of this study. This technology would, however, require 2,635 percent of the labor and 40 percent of the investment of the technology using the least of each of these factors.

b. The technology using the least of this factor was not using any of it.

technology employs ten or more times the amount of semiskilled labor than the most capital-intensive one. This has important social implications, since semiskilled workers can be recruited as unskilled labor and trained on the job. Also, developing countries with a labor surplus generally have this surplus in the unskilled portion of their labor force. At the same time the most labor-intensive technologies only require relatively small increases in supervisory and skilled labor. In fact the technology using the most total labor is often the one that uses the least of one of the high-skill components of the labor force, such as skilled or supervisory labor. In five of the seven processing steps the technologies using the most labor are also the ones using the smallest number of skilled (maintenance) workers. This finding is important since skilled workers are generally scarce in developing countries even though there might be an overall labor surplus.

The most capital-intensive technologies have a larger share of their capital requirement in equipment and a smaller one in buildings. In five processing steps the most capital-intensive technology actually uses less building space per unit of output than the more labor-intensive ones. The resulting savings in building costs at the expense of increased investment in machinery has negative implications for developing countries. In these countries the foreign-exchange component of building costs is generally smaller than that of equipment cost. Furthermore equipment required by labor-intensive technologies is generally simpler than that of capital-intensive ones, and therefore a larger portion of it can be manufactured locally. For these two reasons it can be expected that a smaller percentage of the investment cost of labor-intensive technologies will be in the form of foreign exchange than for capital-intensive ones. The significance of this finding is underscored by the relative scarcity of foreign exchange in developing countries.

Factor Usage in the Pulp and Paper Industry

In the pulp and paper industry a different approach was required to quantify the input requirements of alternative technologies. Technological alternatives available for the main pieces of processing equipment and for the control function were analyzed separately for the reasons given previously.

It was found that a precise quantification of the input requirement of alternative technologies for the main pieces of processing equipment was not possible. The fundamental reason is that in this industry, equipment—with the exception of a few standardized machines such as refiners—must be tailor made. To obtain quotations and input requirements for alternatives requires a large amount of engineering work, which equipment manufacturers are ready to undertake only if it has the potential of yielding orders. The number of units of each category manufactured in a given time period is also too small to allow for any reliable historical analysis of prices. Small differences in the characteristics of the wood processed or in the price of the chemicals used also require important changes in equipment design, thus making quantified comparisons of the main processing equipment used in different plants all but impossible.

The analysis, however, confirmed that the choice between alternative technologies available for the main pieces of processing equipment was made on purely technical grounds. Although such a choice might have a residual impact on labor usage, employment was not a significant variable in the evaluation of alternatives. The data collected showed that the significant capital-labor trade-offs resided in the choice of the control technology rather than in the choice of the main processing equipment technology.

The input requirements of alternative control technologies were collected under the assumption that the same control technology would be used for an entire section of the mill. Although this does not need to be the case in practice, such an assumption yields a better image of the range of factor usage embodied in the spectrum of alternatives. The investment cost of the alternative control technologies was measured as a percentage of the cost of the processing equipment on which these controls were to be installed. An idea of the magnitudes involved and range of factor usage available can be obtained from the summary in table 2.5.

As in the case of the textile industry, these figures show that a wide range of factor usage is available to decision makers. The most labor-intensive technology requires more than seven times the number of operators necessary for the most capital-intensive one. The ratio between the capital usage of the most capital-intensive technology and the most labor-intensive one is the same. It is important to stress that for a pulp mill such as the one described, the operators of the control equipment are the only workers employed in the mill except for maintenance personnel.

Table 2.5
Comparison of Factor Requirements of Alternative Technologies for Control of Operations in a Pulp Mill

	Alternative 1	Alternative 2	Alternative 3	Alternative 4	Alternative 5	Alternative 6	Alternative 7
Cost of instruments and control equipment (as % of total equipment cost)	1.0	2.0	2.5	3.5	4.0	5.0	7.5
Labor usage (per shift)	15	13	10	9	7	4	2

3   The Textile Industry: Production Cost Minimization and Technology Choice

Among the alternative technologies available for each production step in the textile industry, which ones were chosen for developing country facilities? How do the technologies that were chosen compare with those that would have minimized production cost under the prevalent factor price conditions? How do these technologies compare to those that would have been optimal from the country's point of view?

Economists and business persons agree that if alternative technologies utilize the factors of production in different proportions, the "rational" decision maker should choose the technology that minimizes production cost. They might actually disagree when they compute production costs, however, for they use two different sets of prices to represent the cost of the factors of production.

For the economist the prices of the factors of production should reflect their marginal opportunity cost. The choices of technology that minimize costs of production as computed on the basis of such economic (or social) prices for the factors of production should then lead to full employment of these factors in the economy. The cost-minimizing technology at social prices should therefore be considered the social optimum.

For the business person the cost of the factors of production is measured differently. It is what he or she must pay to secure the use of these factors. Such market prices—that is, after all, what they are— should be the same as the social prices if one assumes that a free and perfect market exists for these factors. In most developing countries, however, market imperfections and government intervention tend to distort market prices from their social values. Therefore the business person whose aim is cost minimization will choose the technology that minimizes production costs at the market price of the factors of production. This technology may or may not be the same as the social optimum technology.

For each of the production steps of the production facilities studied, the social optimum technology and the market optimum technology will be identified. The technology actually chosen in these production facilities will then be compared to these optima. A fourth technology, the U.S. technology (the technology that would minimize production cost at U.S. factor prices), is introduced in this comparison. When compared to the technology most adapted to developing countries' conditions, the U.S. technology may be thought of as the choice of a decision maker who would not have been influenced in any way by the local cost of the factors of production.

The fact is that firms do appear to adapt their technology choices to the market prices of the factors of production: of the 110 technology choices in developing countries made by the sixteen textile producers studied, 70 percent were for a technology that was either the market optimum or somewhere between the market optimum and the U.S. technology. Yet this adaptation was not total in nearly 45 percent of these cases since a technology yielding higher production costs than the market optimum was chosen. The choice of a less-than-optimal technology yielded an increase in capital requirements of more than 50 percent and a reduction in employment created of more than a third over that which would have resulted from the optimal choice.

Further economic costs resulted from the fact that factor price distortions caused market prices to be unrepresentative of factor availability in the countries studied. Factor price distortions caused the market optimum technology to differ from the social optimum technology in nearly 50 percent of the cases studied. The macroeconomic consequences of such distortions were important: the market optimum technology generated 45 percent less employment and used 40 percent more capital than the social optimum technology.

Computing the Cost of Using Each Alternative Technology

According to economic theory if alternative technologies using certain factors of production in different combinations are available for the production of a certain good, the choice made among these alternatives should be based solely on the cost of the factors. It should aim at maximizing the return from those factors of production that are supplied by the decision maker. In this study alternative technologies have been defined as those capable of producing an output of similar characteristics. Therefore the output of any of these alternatives should command the same market price, and the project's revenues should be identical whatever the technology chosen. This means that if the impact of corporate taxes is disregarded, a ranking of alternative technologies in terms of production cost should be identical to a ranking in terms of profitability. Because of large variations in the value of textile cloth over time as well as from country to country, this study is based on a comparison of production costs rather than of profits.

Production Costs

A full cost of production computation should include the cost of the raw materials, as well as the cost of all inputs used in the transformation process. This should include machine wear, cost of capital invested in machines, indirect costs, and a portion of overhead costs. Because of the large fluctuations in the price of cotton and artificial fibers during the 1970s and in order to avoid having to choose an arbitrary price for such raw materials, the cost of raw materials was excluded from the cost computations. In the countries where production facilities were studied, however, the price of cotton and artificial fibers remained equal or close to international prices during the 1970s. Therefore all of the firms investigated encountered similar, if not identical, price levels for their raw materials and had a similar incentive to save on raw material usage. The exclusion of raw material costs makes the underlying assumption that raw material wastage would be equal among the alternative technologies. Appendix E provides a critical evaluation of the consequences of this assumption.

Transformation Costs

The comparisons of alternative technologies are based on their estimated transformation costs rather than on full production costs. Transformation costs differ from full production costs in that they exclude raw materials cost and include only indirect costs traceable to the transformation process. Maintenance costs and lighting and air-conditioning of the space in which the transformation occurs are included in the transformation costs; other costs such as administrative expenses are not.

To compare the cost of transformation using alternative technologies, the stream of costs incurred during the life of the equipment should be discounted. This allows for a consideration of variations in some of the cost components—such as maintenance—over the life of the equipment. The difficulty of accurately evaluating the evolution of such costs over time, and imprecision as well as controversy over what should be the rate of discount used, however, make this methodology impractical. Therefore it was decided to use normal year transformation cost, rather than discounted transformation cost as the criterion to compare technologies.

Reliable data on the evolution over the life of a project of cost items such as maintenance and workers' productivity cannot be obtained from either equipment manufacturers or producing firms. Since such data depend upon firm-specific information about preventive maintenance and workers' skill, equipment manufacturers are not able to generate them. Producing firms, on the other hand, do not keep records of such variables or do so in a form that does not permit interfirm comparisons. Furthermore it was found that the firms studied did not incorporate projections of the evolution of maintenance costs in their evaluation of alternative production technologies. Omitting these data would therefore better replicate the information on which the decision makers based their choices.

The cost of transformation was computed for what may be called a normal year of operation. This means a year in which the equipment under study operated at full capacity for the normal number of operating hours per year of this specific plant, and with an adequate supply of all of the factors of production.

Technology Equivalence Coefficients

A comparison of the transformation costs that would have been incurred by a production facility if it were to use each of the alternative technologies requires a determination of the number of units of machinery of each technology that this plant would have needed to produce the same quantity and quality of output. For each technology the number of units required was computed by multiplying the number of units of the technology currently used by an equivalence coefficient between the two technologies. Since this coefficient is to reflect the actual processing capacity of a unit of each alternative, it was designed to reflect the critical element by which processing capacity is measured in that step. This element might be the average weight processed per hour by a unit of each technology, as in the case of carding or drawing, or the degree of uniformity of the mix obtained by each technology, as in the case of plucking. In the case of weaving it would be the number of yards of filling inserted per hour, including all stops while keeping comparable breakage rates.

The equivalence coefficients therefore were evaluated in terms of the capacity of machines of different technologies to perform the type and amount of input transformation required of a processing step rather than in terms of these machines' nominal capacity. For example, in the plucking step textile engineers agree that four manually fed pluckers are required to process 1,000 pounds per hour of cotton, despite the fact that each of these pluckers has a nominal capacity of about 1,000 pounds per hour. The reason for such underutilization of capacity is that using only one unit at full capacity would not provide a fiber mix that is uniform enough to prevent problems in the processing steps that follow and ensure against low quality. On the other hand, if automatic pluckers are used, engineers specify that only two units are needed to process 1,000 pounds per hour satisfactorily. This is because of the better mixing capabilities of these machines, even though each of these units has only a nominal capacity of 500 pounds per hour. In this study the equivalence coefficient between these two technologies was considered to be one automatic plucker to two hand-fed pluckers, rather than the two automatic to one hand-fed that would have resulted from a comparison of nominal capacities.

Exclusion of Duties and Corporate Profit Taxes

Equipment costs were obtained from equipment manufacturers and therefore do not include import duties in the country of destination. Since all of the firms in the sample were exempted from duties on imported equipment, this exclusion will have no bearing on the conclusions of the study.

Comparing transformation costs rather than after-tax discounted cash flow prevents consideration of the effect of corporate taxes on the choice-of-technology decision. Such an omission—which might bias the conclusions in favor of more capital-intensive alternatives—should have had a negligible impact on the resuts of this study. This is because all of the firms studied were granted tax exemptions on their profits for two to five years after start-up, and the impact of taxes in the following years would have had to be discounted to the construction year. As evidence supporting this assertion, none of the companies studied included tax computations in their evaluation of alternative technologies.

Economic Life of Machinery and Buildings

Although equipment and building costs should be allocated to each year of use according to their true economic life, standard economic lives of ten years for equipment and twenty years for buildings were used. Neither equipment manufacturers nor textile producers were able to specify differences in the economic lives of alternative technologies.

Machine Efficiency

It was assumed that a given production facility would reach the same level of machine efficiency if it incorporated the alternative technologies considered as it would with the technology currently used. Machine efficiency is defined here as the ratio of output to machine capacity. The limitations brought about by such an assumption were minimized by taking into account all of the technology-induced inefficiencies in estimating a machine's actual production capacity. For example, the average time a machine has to wait to be manually loaded was taken into consideration in the evaluation of the machine capacity of the manual loading alternative.

Labor Efficiency

The manning requirements of each of the alternative technologies considered were estimated by multiplying the equipment manufacturers' recommended manning tables by a labor efficiency coefficient specific to each firm. This coefficient was estimated by comparing the manufacturer's recommended manning figures for the technology currently in use with the firm's actual manning figures.

The use of the same labor efficiency coefficient for all skill levels and all alternative technologies makes the assumption that labor efficiency does not change according to skill level and to degree of sophistication of the equipment used. Since the managers of the firms studied were of the opinion that labor efficiency in developing countries varies inversely to the level of skill required by the task to be performed, such an assumption might tend to work to the detriment of labor-intensive technologies.

Preventive Versus Corrective Maintenance

The estimated transformation costs include preventive maintenance costs, as well as the cost of parts to be replaced because of normal wear. They do not include corrective maintenance costs.

Under normal operation and with an adequately trained work force, the preventive maintenance costs that are provided for are such as to practically eliminate the need for corrective maintenance. Therefore only firms neglecting preventive maintenance should require substantial amounts of corrective maintenance, and the costs then incurred can be estimated to be equal to the savings realized on preventive maintenance.

Raw Material Wastage and Cost of Defective Products

The rates of raw material wastage and of defective products were assumed to be the same for all alternative technologies. Raw material wastage and the quantity of defective output can be a function of either the quality of the raw material or of machine and worker imprecision and error. In the first case it is normal to assume that wastage rates and defective product rates would be independent of the technology used. In the second case such an assumption is more difficult to make. However, it was found that more capital-intensive equipment, although more precise, also requires better maintenance and tuning, which are difficult to secure in developing countries. Therefore the net effect on raw material wastage and quantity of defective output of these characteristics will be negligible.

Working Capital Needs

Working capital requirements were not included in the capital costs of alternative technologies. Labor-intensive technologies normally would require more working capital than capital-intensive ones because of higher operating costs. Spare parts costs and spare parts inventories, however, were found to be larger in developing countries than in developed ones. They also tend to increase with the degree of capital intensity of the equipment selected. The increase in working capital required to keep a spare parts inventory for more capital-intensive technologies was found to offset the decrease in working capital requirements that results from the smaller wage costs incurred from the use of such technologies.

Cost of Capital

The value of an increase or a decrease in capital cost requirements resulting from the choice of one technology over another should be determined by using the marginal cost of capital to the firm. Because of the unavailability of data required to compute marginal costs of capital, average costs of capital were used instead. This substitution of average for marginal cost of capital should not change the ranking of alternative technologies; it should only reduce differences in their computed costs of transformation.

Sources and Characteristics of the Data Used

Table 3.1 lists the information collected in each of the three main categories: equipment data, production facility data, and country data. The last column shows the cost items included in the transformation cost computations.

During the data collection period (1976–1978), there were few variations in equipment prices. Therefore the specific date at which these prices were collected is not likely to have influenced the results. The equipment prices are f.o.b. and do not include shipment costs, price rebates, and erection costs. Manufacturers' rebates on the price of the equipment were found to offset roughly the cost of transportation and installation.

Production facility data were corrected for unusual operating circumstances such as plants that were operating much below normal levels because of market circumstances. Since the values of some of the parameters measured might have changed since the time the choices of technology were made (1970–1975), it was verified that such changes would not have introduced a systematic bias in the results of this study. Changes in relative prices did not take place in this period except for the cost of energy, a relatively small cost item in the textile process. Changes in exchange rates were also found to have been roughly in line with differential rates of inflation.

Social cost computations were based on a set of shadow prices generated from World Bank information. World Bank economists estimate shadow prices for each of the member developing countries for use in the Bank's evaluation of projects. Although these shadow prices incorporate some subjectivity in the choice of a methodology as well as in the estimation of certain parameters, they do possess the advantage

Table 3.1
Computation of Transformation Costs

Equipment Data	Production Facility Data	Country Data	Transformation Cost Items
Cost per unit	Number of units required	Social depreciation period equipment	Annual depreciation equipment
Floor area per unit	Depreciation period equipment	Social depreciation period buildings	Annual depreciation buildings
Spare parts requirement per unit	Depreciation period buildings	Social cost of construction	Annual cost of capital
Power requirement per unit	Cost of construction/ sq. m.	Social cost of capital	Annual cost of spare parts
Labor requirement per unit	Cost of capital	Social cost of power	Annual cost of power, equipment
Supervisory	Cost of power	Optimum number of shifts	Annual cost of power, lighting
Skilled	No. of shifts working	Optimum number of hours worked per week	Annual cost of power, air-conditioning
Semiskilled	No. of hours worked per year	Country's labor efficiency	Annual cost of labor
Unskilled	Labor efficiency factor	Social cost of labor	Supervisory
% of unit cost procured locally	Cost of labor	Supervisory	Skilled
Colombia	Supervisory	Skilled	Semiskilled
Brazil	Skilled	Semiskilled	Unskilled
Philippines	Semiskilled	Unskilled	
Indonesia	Unskilled	Shadow foreign exchange conversion factor	

of having been derived in a consistent manner for each country. Table 3.2 provides the shadow prices used in this study.

The techniques used to derive these shadow prices as well as a more detailed description of the model, its assumptions, and its limitations can be found in appendix E.

Overall Results of Transformation Cost Comparisons

The transformation cost that would have resulted from the use of each of the alternative technologies was computed for the seven processing steps in the nineteen textile plants covered by this study. These computations were conducted at the market and at the social prices of the factors of production in each case. Although the results of these computations enable comparisons to be made of alternative technologies within a given company, they cannot be used to make direct comparisons between companies. The reason is that the transformation costs computed are for the specific volume of production and output mix (in terms of yarn size, construction of cloth, and so forth) of each production facility. Therefore these figures will need to be adjusted before interfacility comparisons can be made.

The technology that yields the lowest transformation cost at market prices for each processing step in each production facility will be referred to as the market optimum. The technology that results in the lowest transformation cost at social prices of the factors of production, will be termed the social optimum.

Table 3.3 identifies the market optimum, the social optimum, and the technology chosen for each step of the production process of the nineteen facilities studied. Thus it summarizes the results of the transformation cost computations.

Figure 3.1 presents these results in visual form as technology profiles.[1] Together with the technology profile of the facility considered it presents the technology profile that would have resulted in the lowest financial (market) transformation cost for this facility and the technology profile that would have resulted in the lowest social cost of production for the country. The profile of the optimum technology (both financially and socially) for the U.S. market has been included for the purpose of comparison. The profile of the financially optimal alternative might change from facility to facility in the same country, depending upon the price paid for the factors of production by each firm and upon its

Table 3.2
Social Prices Used

	Colombia	Brazil, south	Brazil, northeast	Philippines	Indonesia	Japan and United States
Capital (%)	10	14	14	12	15	Market prices used
Labor (U.S.$ per day)						
Supervisory	8.04	32.00	20.10	6.36	4.50	
Skilled	5.30	14.64	10.00	3.29	2.79	
Semiskilled	1.15	2.50	1.53	0.60	0.50	
Unskilled	1.15	2.50	1.53	0.60	0.50	
Labor efficiency (%)	70	75	75	60	70	
Power (U.S.¢/kwh)	3.5	3.0	3.0	3.0	8.0	
Construction cost (U.S.$/sq. m.)	110	200	200	106	210	
% of building cost in foreign exchange	25	15	15	30	40	
Shadow foreign exchange factor	1.19	1.25	1.25	1.11	1.50	

Table 3.3
Social and Market Optima and Technology Chosen

	Company																		
	1	2	3	4	5	6	7	8	9	10	11	12	13	14	15	16	17	18	19
	Colombia			Brazil		Philippines					Indonesia						Japan		U.S.
Plucking (3 alternatives)																			
Technology chosen	1	1	1	3	3	1	1	1	1	1	1	1	1	1	1	1	2	2	3
Market optimum	1	2	2	2	2	1	2	1	1	2	1	1	1	1	1	1	2	2	2
Social optimum	1	1	1	1	1	1	1	1	1	1	1	1	1	1	1	1	2	2	2
Scutching (5 alternatives)																			
Technology chosen	1	1	1	5	5	1	2	3	2	1	5	2	1	5	3	1	5	4	3
Market optimum	1	5	5	5	1	1	1	1	1	1	1	1	1	1	1	1	5	5	5
Social optimum	1	1	1	1	1	1	1	1	1	1	1	1	1	1	1	1	5	5	5
Carding (7 alternatives)																			
Technology chosen	3	1	4	5	6	1	5	3	4	2	5	3	1	3	3	2	7	6	6
Market optimum	2	2	2	2	2	2	2	2	2	2	2	2	2	2	2	2	2	2	5
Social optimum	2	2	2	2	2	2	2	2	2	2	2	2	2	2	2	2	2	2	5
Drawing (4 alternatives)																			
Technology chosen	2	2	2	2	2	2	2	1	1	1	2	3	2	2	2	2	4	4	3
Market optimum	1	2	2	2	2	1	2	1	1	2	2	2	2	2	2	2	2	2	4
Social optimum	1	1	1	2	1	1	1	1	1	1	1	1	1	1	1	1	2	2	4

Winding (8 alternatives)																		
Technology chosen	3	2	3	4	4	1	1	3	2	1	1	1	1	3	1	8	8	8
Market optimum	2	3	3	3	2	2	2	1	2	1	1	1	1	2	1	3	3	8
Social optimum	1	1	1	1	1	1	1	1	1	1	1	1	1	1	1	3	3	8
Pirn winding (4 alternatives)																		
Technology chosen	2	2	2	4	4	2	2	2	2		3	2	3	3	2	3	3	
Market optimum	2	3	3	3	3	2	2	2	3		2	2	2	2	2	3	3	
Social optimum	2	2	2	2	2	2	2	2	2		2	2	2	2	2	3	3	
Weaving (10 alternatives)																		
Technology chosen	5	5	5	6	6	5	7	5	5		4	4	5	4	4	9	8	9
Market optimum	3	4	4	4	4	3	3	3	4		3	3	4	4	3	4	4	9
Social optimum	3	3	3	3	3	3	3	3	3		3	3	3	3	3	4	4	9

Note: Numbers are technology levels. 1 = most labor-intensive technology.

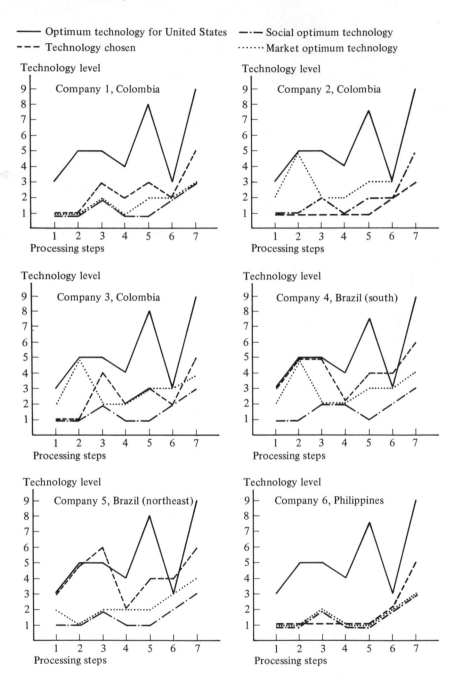

Figure 3.1
The Technology Profiles of the Textile Firms Studied

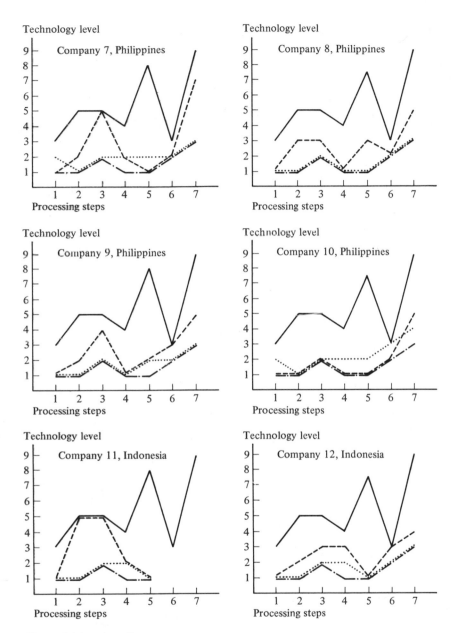

Figure 3.1 (continued)

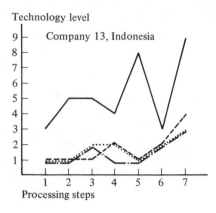

Technology level

Company 13, Indonesia

Processing steps

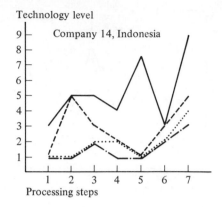

Technology level

Company 14, Indonesia

Processing steps

Technology level

Company 15, Indonesia

Processing steps

Technology level

Company 16, Indonesia

Processing steps

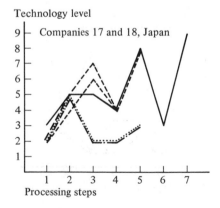

Technology level

Companies 17 and 18, Japan

Processing steps

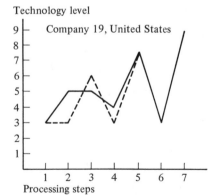

Technology level

Company 19, United States

Processing steps

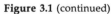

Figure 3.1 (continued)

efficiency. On the other hand the profile of the socially optimal technologies for all firms within a country will remain the same.

The Firm's Adaptation to Local Factor Prices

While market optimum and social optimum technologies were found to differ in nearly half of the cases studied, a private firm cannot be expected to choose the social optimum technology. If minimization of production costs is its sole objective, as assumed by economic theory, a firm would obviously choose the market optimum technology. If it were to choose the social optimum technology, it would in fact incur higher production costs than with the market optimum.

Therefore if one wishes to evaluate the tendency of any firm to adapt to the local price of the factors of production—in other words, to minimize production costs—the technology it chose should be compared to the respective market optimum technologies.

Extent of Adaptation

If firms were not at all influenced by the differences in the cost of the factors of production among countries, one might postulate that they would always choose the most modern proven technology, the one designed to suit best the factor prices of developed countries. The technology best suited to U.S. factor prices is thus defined as the unadapted technology and will be used as a reference point in the following comparisons.

Table 3.4 shows a comparison of the technology actually chosen, the optimum technology at the factor prices paid by the firm, and the corresponding unadapted technology for each observation.

The form in which the results of the transformation cost computations are presented in tables 3.3 and 3.4 and in figure 3.1 has two important shortcomings. First, interprocessing step comparisons are not possible. The amounts of adaptation that took place cannot be compared among steps since the difference in technological level—the basic measurement—is highly dependent upon the number of alternative technologies for each step. Alternative technologies of two steps could also vary widely in their relative requirements of the factors of production and thus in their resulting trasformation cost. Second, intercompany comparisons are not possible. The cost of transformation for two alternative technologies might be quite similar in one firm, thus making the choice

Table 3.4
Technology Chosen, Market Optimum, and U.S. Technology in the Textile Industry

Company[a]	Plucking	Scutching	Carding	Drawing	Winding	Pirn Winding	Weaving	Totals[b] −	=	+	++
1	=	=	+	+	+	=	+	0	3	4	0
2	−	−	−	−	−	−	+	6	0	1	0
3	−	−	+	=	=	−	+	3	2	2	0
4	++	++	++	=	+	++	+	0	2	2	3
5	++	+	++	=	+	++	+	0	1	2	4
6	=	=	−	=	=	=	+	1	5	1	0
7	−	+	++	=	−	=	+	2	2	2	1
8	=	+	+	=	+	=	+	0	3	4	0
9	=	+	+	=	=	++	+	0	3	3	1
10	−	=	=	−	−	−	+	4	2	1	0
11	=	++	++	=	=	None	None	0	3	0	2
12	=	+	+	+	=	++	+	0	2	4	1
13	=	=	−	=	=	=	+	1	5	1	0
14	=	++	+	+	=	++	+	0	3	2	2
15	=	+	+	+	+	++	+	0	1	5	1
16	=	=	=	=	=	=	+	0	6	1	0
Totals, companies 1–16[b]											
−	4	2	3	2	3	3	0	17	-	-	-
=	10	6	2	11	8	6	0	-	43	-	-

+	0	5	7	3	5	0	15	–	–	35	–
++	2	3	4	0	0	6	)	–	–	–	15
17	=	=	++	++	++	None	++	0	2	0	4
18	=	–	++	++	++	None	+	1	1	1	3
19	+	–	+	–	=	None	=	2	2	2	–

a. Companies 1–16 are in developing countries; companies 17–19 are in developed countries.

b. Number of cases in the corresponding line or column in which each of the types of technology choices was observed.

− Technology chosen less automated than market optimum. + Technology chosen between market optimum and U.S. technology.

= Technology chosen is market optimum. ++Technology chosen is U.S. technology or is more automated than it.

of technology relatively unimportant. Yet in another firm, the transformation costs of the same technologies might be quite different, making the choice between them more critical.

Propensity to Adapt

A propensity to adapt index was created in an effort to reflect these considerations. Conceptually it is a measure of how close a firm came to minimizing its transformation cost when it chose a technology for a particular production step. Through its choice of a technology, a firm realizes a portion of the transformation cost savings that its market optimum technology would have provided over the U.S. technology.

A firm's propensity to adapt for a given production step is expressed as the percentage of the potential transformation cost savings of the optimum technology as compared to the U.S. technology that the chosen technology realized over the U.S. technology. All production costs— of the U.S. technology, the optimum technology, and the technology chosen—are computed at the cost of the factors of production encountered by the firms whose propensity to adapt is being evaluated.

Propensity to Adapt Index

A propensity to adapt index can therefore be derived for each choice of technology made by a firm—in other words, for each production step. If a firm chooses the optimum technology, its propensity to adapt index will be 100 for this production step. If it chooses the U.S. technology, its propensity to adapt index will equal 0.

This index is derived as follows:

$$\text{propensity to adapt} = \frac{\text{TC US Tech.} - \text{TC Chosen Tech.}}{\text{TC US Tech.} - \text{TC Optimum Tech.}} \times 100$$

where TC US Tech. is the transformation cost obtained by using the technology that is optimum at the U.S. cost of the factors of production; TC Chosen Tech. is the transformation cost obtained using the technology chosen; and TC Optimum Tech. is the minimum transformation cost that can be obtained through the use of any of the technologies available.

This formula can be adapted so that the computation can be made under market or social conditions. The applicable formula under market conditions is:

propensity to adapt
$$= \frac{\text{TC MPF US Tech.} - \text{TC MPF Chosen Tech.}}{\text{TC MPF US Tech} - \text{TC MPF Market Opt. Tech.}} \times 100,$$

where TC MPF is the transformation cost at market price of the factors. Under social conditions it is:

propensity to adapt
$$= \frac{\text{TC SPF US Tech.} - \text{TC SPF Chosen Tech.}}{\text{TC SPF US Tech.} - \text{TC SPF Social Opt. Tech.}} \times 100,$$

where TC SPF is the transformation cost at social price of the factors. (Appendix D gives the values of these ratios for each processing step of each company.)

Tables 3.5 and 3.6 summarize these findings by giving the average values of these indexes for each processing step and each production facility in the sample. Following the propensity to adapt and the cost due to distortions indexes, the ratio of the chosen technology's requirement of each main factor of production over the optimum technology requirement is given.

Table 3.7 furnishes an overall summary of the results of the cost of transformation comparisons of the market optimum technologies and the technologies chosen by the firms studied.

Conclusions

1. When production technologies are chosen for textile manufacturing in developing countries, a large amount of adaptation to the factor cost structure of the country does indeed take place. This is evidenced by the dissimilarity between the technology profiles of the U.S. technology and those of the firms from developing countries in our study (see figure 3.1). In 95 of this study's 110 technology observations in developing countries (86 percent of the cases) the technology chosen was more labor intensive than the U.S. optimum at identical scale of production (see table 3.4). Of the firms in the sample, the average propensity to adapt varies from 51 to 96, depending upon the processing step, with an average value of 73. This figure is not weighted according to the relative importance of the various processing steps.

Table 3.5
Textile: Extent and Impact of Adaptation, Company Averages (in percentages except for propensity to adapt)

	Company																		
	1	2	3	4	5	6	7	8	9	10	11	12	13	14	15	16	17	18	19
	Colombia		Brazil			Philippines					Indonesia						Japan		U.S.
Propensity to adapt																			
At social prices	79	89	72	42	30	90	64	69	57	94	59	66	94	43	53	97	9	(15)	50
At market prices	85	133	64	58	18	104	55	68	59	89	60	66	103	57	51	99	9	(15)	50
Cost due to distortions	3	44	44	40	25	0	11	0	5	28	1	0	0	3	6	0	0	0	0
Employment Creation																			
Versus social optimum	77	111	75	52	49	119	79	74	76	94	68	95	118	74	70	92	60	141	225
Versus market optimum	92	321	277	90	69	119	123	74	84	145	70	86	119	81	81	94	60	141	225
Loss due to distortions	8	42	42	40	25	0	18	0	8	26	2	1	1	7	15	1	0	0	0
Employment supervisory and skilled																			
Versus social optimum	87	107	82	87	87	111	88	91	90	97	81	96	111	90	94	95	86	106	116
Versus market optimum	90	131	105	100	93	111	103	91	95	111	84	99	113	95	102	97	86	106	116
Loss due to distortions	5	13	17	15	7	0	11	0	5	9	3	2	2	4	9	2	0	0	0

Employment semiskilled and unskilled																			
Versus social optimum	76	113	74	48	45	121	77	72	74	93	66	82	120	72	67	92	56	564	933
Versus market optimum	80	302	240	88	65	121	128	72	82	153	68	83	121	79	79	93	56	564	933
Loss due to distortions	8	35	45	43	27	0	19	0	8	27	2	1	1	7	16	1	0	0	0
Capital requirement																			
Versus social optimum	136	138	140	184	187	125	146	157	152	113	124	115	116	125	148	104	144	147	101
Versus market optimum	120	102	101	138	154	125	133	157	126	90	124	115	116	120	117	104	144	147	101
Increase due to distortions	14	43	43	38	22	0	30	0	26	38	0	0	0	4	26	0	0	0	0
Equipment requirement																			
Versus social optimum	147	147	153	225	230	132	166	172	167	121	134	122	121	142	167	111	160	165	102
Versus market optimum	128	101	103	154	175	132	151	172	135	90	132	121	120	127	119	109	160	165	102
Increase due to distortions	16	54	54	52	35	0	39	0	31	50	2	2	2	11	42	2	0	0	0
Building requirement																			
Versus social optimum	99	109	93	77	74	112	95	102	93	97	86	101	110	94	103	95	92	96	124
Versus market optimum	103	117	98	79	83	112	102	102	96	106	91	105	114	99	113	99	92	96	124
Increase due to distortions	(3)	(3)	(3)	1	(6)	0	(7)	0	(3)	(6)	(5)	(4)	(4)	(5)	(8)	(4)	0	0	0

Table 3.5 (Continued)

	Company																		
	1	2	3	4	5	6	7	8	9	10	11	12	13	14	15	16	17	18	19
	Colombia			Brazil		Philippines					Indonesia						Japan		U.S.
Foreign exchange requirement																			
Versus social optimum	143	144	149	583	583	129	158	166	161	118	129	118	118	133	158	107	0	0	0
Versus market optimum	125	150	151	313	358	129	144	166	132	90	128	117	117	123	118	106	0	0	0
Increase due to distortions	15	35	35	251	197	0	36	0	30	59	1	1	1	7	34	1	0	0	0

Note: See note in appendix D.
Source: Appendix D.

2. In about a third of the cases, the firms in the sample chose a technology that was positioned between the U.S. and the market optimum technologies in terms of labor intensity. If one considers only those cases in which such an intermediate technology was available, the results are even more striking. The intermediate alternative was chosen in more than 40 percent of these cases. This seems to indicate that although firms do in fact respond to differences in factor cost structures in their choice of technology, other factors make them adopt more capital-intensive technologies than those that would minimize transformation cost. These factors will be investigated more closely.

3. In the 45 percent of the observations in which the chosen technology was more capital intensive than the market optimum, the impact of this less-than-optimal choice on capital requirement and employment creation was large. The impact on transformation cost was not as significant.

The choice in 50 cases of a technology that was more capital intensive than the optimum resulted in a combined increase in transformation cost of 22 percent. It provoked a 52 percent increase in capital requirements and a 119 percent increase in the foreign exchange component of this capital requirement. It also resulted in the creation of only 68 percent of the jobs that would have been created had the market optimum technology been selected. In other words the social cost of this less-than-optimum adaptation to local market prices is much greater than its market, or private, cost.

4. In 15 percent of the cases a technology more labor-intensive than the market optimum was chosen. These cases might be called situations of overadaptation. Although they might lead to the choice of a socially more appropriate technology, they are suboptimal choices from the private point of view.

Although some of these choices might be attributable to poor or misinformed decision making, others seem to have an underlying rationale. More than 50 percent of these more labor-intensive-than-optimum choices were encountered in two of the three Columbian firms studied. The third firm was the industry leader. The reason for these overadaptive choices seems to be that interest rates in Colombia were kept artificially low, thus resulting in low capital cost and relatively more capital-intensive market optima. Capital shortages resulting from these artificial prices, however, brought about a capital rationing situation. The two nonindustry leaders encountered more difficulty in obtaining capital than did the industry leader and as a result chose

Table 3.6
Textile: Extent and Impact of Adaptation, Processing Step Averages (in percentages except for propensity to adapt)

	Plucking (1)	Scutching (2)	Carding (3)	Drawing (4)	Winding (5)	Pirn winding (6)	Weaving (7)
Propensity to adapt							
At social prices	88	60	40	94	75	45	52
At market prices	80	51	65	96	87	60	55
Cost due to distortion	15	19	0	3	19	33	5
Employment created							
Versus social optimum	92	70	102	93	65	98	59
Versus market optimum	142	214	102	99	107	103	74
Loss due to distortion	24	17	0	7	35	4	17
Employment supervisory-skilled							
Versus social optimum	98	92	101	91	79	117	79
Versus market optimum	112	103	101	101	101	109	84
Loss due to distortion	11	7	0	9	21	(7)	5
Employment semiskilled-unskilled							
Versus social optimum	91	67	102	93	64	97	56
Versus market optimum	152	1,054	102	99	107	102	73
Loss due to distortion	26	19	0	6	36	4	19
Capital requirement							
Versus social optimum	106	127	142	104	181	123	176
Versus market optimum	97	117	142	102	111	116	155

Increase due to distortion	10	15	0	2	79	5	15
Equipment requirement							
Versus social optimum	111	135	146	109	197	128	237
Versus market optimum	97	123	146	102	113	121	192
Increase due to distortion	15	18	0	8	97	5	28
Buildings requirement							
Versus social optimum	100	93	117	84	105	91	80
Versus market optimum	100	99	117	105	106	89	82
Increase due to distortion	0	(5)	0	(19)	(4)	5	(3)
Foreign exchange requirement							
Versus social optimum	268	155	145	107	252	205	214
Versus market optimum	97	132	145	102	115	164	316
Increase due to distortion	134	29	0	5	130	10	(6)

Note: See appendix C.
Source: Appendix C.

Table 3.7
Choice of Technology Made by Firms in Sample and Its Impact on Input Requirements

Technology Chosen	More Labor Intensive than Market Optimum	Market Optimum	Between Market Optimum and U.S. Technology	U.S. Technology	More Capital Intensive than U.S. Technology
Number of observations	17	43	35	12	3
% of total number of observations	15	39	32	11	3
Input requirements (average % increase or decrease over market optimum requirements)[a]					
Transformation cost	+19	0	+17	+6	+51
Employment	+225	0	−29	−36	−8
Supervisory and skilled	+42	0	−14	−9	+22
Semiskilled and unskilled	+1,033	0	−32	−40	−12
Capital requirement	−8	0	+48	+33	+103
Equipment	−12	0	+68	+43	+133
Buildings	+26	0	0	−8	−72
Foreign exchange	−11	0	+125	+39	+361

a. The figures in this table are averages of the percentage increase or decrease over market optimum requirements that each choice of technology resulted in. In these averages, the observations are not weighted according to the relative importance of the processing steps or companies.

technologies that were more labor intensive than those that would have been dictated by the official cost of capital to the firm.

An analysis of the technologies chosen by the developed countries' firms for their home country facilities is outside the scope of this study. However, some interesting comments can be made on this subject even though they are based on a very small number of observations. The two Japanese firms tended to choose technologies for their home country facilities that were much more capital intensive than their market optima. This was true in eight out of twelve cases. In seven of these eight more capital-intensive decisions, the technology chosen was as capital intensive as, or more so than, the U.S. optimum technology. The American firm, on the other hand, tended to make choices that were slightly less capital intensive than its market optima and therefore seemed to lag in the adoption of the technology that would minimize its production cost. In two of the six cases, the technology chosen by this American firm was more labor intensive than the optimum.

The Impact of Factor Price Distortions: Market Optimum Versus Social Optimum

In 46 percent of the observations, distortions in factor prices caused the social optimum technology to differ from the optimum technology for the firm.

Although distortions in factor prices existed and were significant in all of the developing countries covered by the study, the noncontinuous nature of the range of available technology alternatives caused the social and market optima to still coincide in a slight majority of the cases.

The difference that exists between the social transformation cost of the market optimum technology and of the social optimum technology should be viewed as the social cost of distortions in the cost of factors of production. If one divides this social cost of distortions by the social savings that would result from the choice of the social optimum technology over the U.S. technology, a valuable measure is obtained: the measure of the portion of the social savings made possible by a full adaptation to factor availability, which are lost because of factor price distortions. In mathematical form, this can be expressed through the following formula:

cost of distortions index

$$= \frac{\text{TC SPF Market Opt. Tech.} - \text{TC SPF Social Opt. Tech.}}{\text{TC SPF US Tech.} - \text{TC SPF Social Opt. Tech.}} \times 100.$$

In appendix D and in summary tables 3.5 and 3.6, cost of distortion indexes are shown under the heading "cost due to distortions." The lines labeled "loss due to distortions" and "increase due to distortions" indicate the percentage increase or decrease in utilization of each of the main factors of production that the market optimum technology represents over the social optimum one.

In cases where the market optimum and the social optimum were different, the differences in the employment effect of the two technologies were large. This makes distortions in factor prices a powerful explanatory variable of suboptimal employment creation from the social point of view. In the fifty-one cases where the market optimum technology and the social optimum technology were different, an increase of 82 percent in employment creation would have resulted from an adoption of the social optimum rather than the market optimum. At the same time a reduction of 32 percent in capital requirement and of 18 percent in the foreign exchange requirement would have occurred.

Surprisingly the reduction in foreign exchange requirement is smaller than the overall reduction in capital requirement. This result is brought about by several observations in Colombia and Brazil. In these cases equipment embodying the market optimum technology was manufactured locally, while equipment embodying the more labor-intensive social optimum was not. The locally manufactured equipment was not found to be socially optimum even though the smaller foreign exchange requirement it represented was taken into account. These cases illustrate the impact that the local production of some of the alternative technologies can have on the choice made by manufacturing firms. Also demonstrated is the often-neglected role that governments of developing countries may play in promoting the use of labor-intensive technologies by encouraging domestic production of labor-intensive equipment.

If one excludes situations where equipment more capital intensive than the social optimum was produced locally, the reduction in foreign exchange requirement that would have resulted from a shift from market to social optima would have been 43 percent instead of 18 percent.

4

The Textile Industry: Non-Factor-Price Considerations in Technology Choice

Since more capital-intensive than cost-minimizing technologies were chosen, what are the considerations, other than factor prices, that influence the technology choices of textile producers in developing countries? How were these choice-of-technology decisions made?

Non-Factor-Price Considerations: The Evidence

It is clear that the firms under study adapted their technology choices, to some extent, to the costs of the factors of production they were encountering. This was shown by their choice of technologies that were more labor intensive than the technologies that were actually most suited to a developed country's conditions. In the majority of cases, however, their adaptation did not extend to selecting the technologies best suited to the relative availability of the factors of production in the country. Although distortions in factor prices explain part of this gap, they do not explain all of it. In nearly half of the cases the technology chosen continued to be more capital intensive than the technology that would have minimized production cost at prevalent market prices.

Furthermore the technologies chosen were not uniformly more capital intensive than the market optimum technology. The gap between the market optimum technology and the technology chosen seemed instead to depend upon characteristics of the firm that made the choice, the country in which the production facility was to operate, and the step in the production process for which the choice was made.

These observations point to the existence of considerations other than transformation cost minimization in the technology choice decision. Numerous studies devoted to this subject have yielded results that are difficult to reconcile, if not outright contradictory.[1] Nevertheless, these studies were the source of many of the hypotheses underlying this investigation. Wherever possible, similarities and differences between the conclusions of previous studies and this one will be explained.

The weight each consideration had in the choice-of-technology decision can be discerned by analyzing the position of the chosen technology in relation to the cost-minimizing technology and the U.S. technology—in other words by its impact on the firm's propensity to adapt. A statistical identification and weighting of the variables explaining variations in a firm's propensity to adapt is theoretically possible. The relatively small number of observations (110 observations in 19 firms), however, precludes this; therefore only simple statistical measures will be used. Findings may be considered indicative of tendencies rather than as precise evaluations of the considerations influencing the decisions.

The Decision Process

A high degree of similarity in the decision process leading to technology choices existed among the textile firms investigated. The limited variations identified were found to be related to their pattern of ownership, the country in which the production facility was located, or the production step for which a technology was chosen. These variations occurred in the weight given to the different stages or factors in the decision process rather than in the form of the decision process itself.

The three stages of the decision process are shown in figure 4.1. Each production step can be considered a separate choice of a technology.

Stage One: Identification of the Alternatives

The first step consisted of compiling a list of pieces of equipment considered to be viable alternatives for performing the processing step under study. This was not a list of alternative technologies as defined so far nor a list of machines embodying the same technology but manufactured by different equipment suppliers. Instead the list most often included both alternative technologies and alternative versions of the same technology. Characteristically three or four equipment manufacturers and one to three models from each of these equipment suppliers were included.

This list was drawn up by engineers and involved their judgment of what would be viable technological alternatives for the production

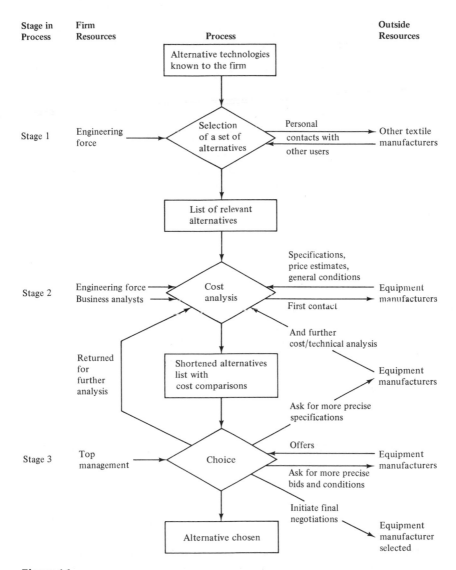

Figure 4.1
Choice-of-Technology Decision Process in the Textile Industry

facility considered. In none of the firms visited did management issue any criteria or guidelines on which these judgments were to be based. The closest thing to management guidelines were instructions to minimize equipment cost as far as possible. A few other firms provided some indications of overall investment costs for the plant, within which engineers had to remain.

When questioned the engineers could not offer any clear criteria that they used to decide whether to exclude or include a technology or manufacturer. "Experience with the manufacturer" and "renown of the manufacturer" were often mentioned. Others were "a well-proven design" or "a widely used technology." Although a set of rational factors appears to underlie these rather vague answers, the lack of clear definition of these criteria made their application difficult to evaluate. In the same way this vagueness must have made it impossible for nonengineers in the firm to challenge that list.

This stage in the decision process, and the way in which it is carried out, seems to condition much of the outcome of the whole process as far as technology choice is concerned. In most cases the list of possibilities contained no more than two or three technological alternatives, although each of them was generally represented by several machines proposed by different equipment manufacturers.

Stage Two: Analysis of the Alternatives

The next stage in the decision process consisted of an evaluation of the cost competitiveness of each of the alternatives proposed. To use a terminology created by Louis T. Wells, this part of the decision process was the one in which the "economic man" looked for the cost-minimizing technology.[2] His search, however, had been limited at the outset to the range of technologies selected by engineers.

The scope and sophistication of the cost analysis varied greatly among firms. In its most rudimentary form it consisted of a simple comparison of the purchase costs of equipment necessary to process the anticipated production volume of the proposed facility. In its most sophisticated form it involved a detailed computation of the cost of production using each of the alternative pieces of equipment, including manning requirements for the different levels of skill required, power costs, spare parts costs, and other factors.

In none of the cases studied did this analysis take the form of a profit analysis in which not only the cost of production but also the value of the output would have had to be estimated. When each production step is studied separately, profit analyses are extremely difficult to perform because of the lack of realistic transfer prices for goods at different stages of processing. Since the technologies compared were to produce an identical output, however, the value of the output of each step would be identical whatever the technology used. The only consequence of comparing transformation costs rather than profits would be to overlook the impact of taxes (and accelerated depreciation) on the relative attractiveness of alternative technologies.

In none of the cases were the cost computations made on a discounted basis. In all cases where cost of transformation rather than investment cost comparisons were made, costs of transformation were estimated for a standard year of operation. For the purpose of these computations all investment costs such as equipment and buildings were allocated on a yearly basis. The computations did not take into account possible differences in the learning curves of the various skills needed from the workers who were to staff the equipment. In addition possible changes in maintenance and spare parts requirements over the life of the equipment were not included. Although in such a model it would be technically possible to take into account differences in the economic life of the various equipment being considered, such forecasts were not made, and instead standardized economic lives were used for all alternative technologies.

The model used in this study to identify the market optimum technology is similar to the most sophisticated versions of cost of production comparisons encountered in the firms investigated. The main difference in this book's use of such a model is that the full spectrum of technological alternatives, rather than just a preselected segment, was probed. In addition the emphasis was on evaluating alternative technologies rather than a mixture of alternative technologies and alternative versions of the same technology.

These cost of production computations were customarily arrived at by engineers in collaboration with business-trained professionals. The role of the engineers was to provide necessary basic data and parameters, which they derived from their experience with the manning, spare parts, maintenance, and power requirements of equipment they had previously used. They also consulted equipment manufacturers' specifications of equipment with which they had had no experience.

It is at this stage that discussions with equipment manufacturers generally began. The equipment manufacturers included in the list compiled by the engineers were contacted by mail or visited. The engineers provided these suppliers with an overall technical description of the project including volume of production, types of products to be manufactured, and characteristics of the raw materials to be used. The equipment manufacturers would then be asked for the technical characteristics of the equipment that they would recommend, as well as their specifications of models and number of units that they felt should be installed. Preliminary price quotations, estimated delivery dates, and financing terms were also solicited from these manufacturers.

If the number of technological alternatives proposed by the engineers was large—five or more—some would be eliminated at this stage in the decision process. Such eliminations were based on pure cost considerations. First equipment costs were considered, then total investment cost (equipment plus building), and finally rough production cost comparisons would be used as criteria for elimination if the number of alternatives was still considered to be too extensive.

By the end of this second stage in the decision process, the number of alternatives being considered for a particular production step would be narrowed to two to four. An economic comparison of a form and level of sophistication customary to the firm making the choice would have been developed between these alternatives.

Stage Three: The Final Choice

Here the alternatives and the cost comparisons that were developed in stage two were transmitted to a management group in charge of making the final choice.

In the case of a small, family-owned firm, this decision-making body might be composed of only the president-owner and the production manager. For a large multinational firm the decision making might be assigned to a formal or informal project committee, generally composed of three or four managers at the department-head level. The production function, the financial function, and the research and development function, if any, would normally be represented in that committee. In none of the cases studied was the final decision left to only one person, although one person might make the final decision if no consensus could be reached.

Together with the economic analysis of the alternatives proposed, a qualitative description of any nonquantifiable or nonquantified elements considered to be important for the decision, as well as a recommendation as to what this decision should be, were forwarded to the decision-making body by those who had performed the analysis. Such qualitative comments customarily dealt with the reputation and reliability of—and previous experience with—the equipment manufacturers included in the list. Other considerations were any previous installations by these manufacturers in the country where the production facility was to be located and the supplier's representation and servicing structure in that country.

The amount of time and attention this decision-making body devoted to a specific choice-of-technology decision seemed to depend mainly upon the relative importance of the processing step studied in the production process and the number of available alternatives, both in terms of technology and in terms of manufacturing sources. No simple measure of the importance of a particular processing step appeared to exist. Rather a composite criterion emerged that took into account the importance of this processing step in determining the quality of the end product as well as the proportion of expenditures this step would contribute to the total equipment cost of the project.

In selecting equipment the warping and sizing steps generally received little attention because only a limited number of technology alternatives existed and because investment cost was low and the machinery was simple. On the other hand the choice of equipment for the opening room and for the spinning step received a great deal of attention. These are highly important production steps, affecting overall quality, and they require a large investment in equipment. Thus despite the fact that a limited number of alternative technologies was available, much attention was given to this selection. The choice of looms always involved painstaking attention because of the importance of the weaving step as well as the large number of alternatives it offers.

At this point the decision process might follow one of several courses. The decision-making body might find the information on hand to be sufficient, allowing for a clear-cut decision. In that case the group would make a definitive choice and initiate final negotiations with the equipment manufacturer selected. Often, however, the decision makers found that a choice was not clear-cut. Either some further analysis was necessary or the decision hinged on a better knowledge of possible rebates and special conditions.

Such a delay was generally found in cases where equipment was under consideration for what were defined as important processing steps. The number of alternative choices would be reduced to two, or a maximum of three, generally from different equipment manufacturers. These alternatives might also embody different technology levels. The remaining two or three alternatives would be referred back to those in charge of the analysis at the preceding stage for further, more sophisticated analysis. Alternatively more precise technical information and formal bids would be requested from the equipment suppliers and the additional information obtained handed to the preceding level for evaluation.

This procedure was sometimes repeated several times, either out of the need for more detailed evaluation of the performance of the equipment or merely in order to promote price competition between the equipment manufacturers. Obviously the larger the company and the larger the order it intended to place, the more it was in a position to adopt this strategy. For example, although the order that a very large American firm was to place to equip a foreign venture was expected to be only of medium size, loom manufacturers went to great lengths to initiate relations—or keep their ongoing business—with such an important customer. Some of them went so far as to send a loom with the characteristics recommended to the company's plant so that the firm's engineers could test it.

The same pattern of voluntary and involuntary commitments as that which was described by Yair Aharoni in his analysis of the foreign investment decision process was encountered in this study. Aharoni pointed out that "during the decision process itself, commitments are created by the very act of investigation." "In order to collect information, it is necessary to communicate with people, to make certain decisions, and often to give tacit promises," some of which are contradictory, creating a conflict that must be resolved.[3] Such conflicts of commitments were often resolved through a bargaining process internal to the firm—between the different individuals or groups that made these commitments. The result of such internal bargaining might then be a compromise that is difficult to explain by a set of logical factors.

Standardization of Choices

Each step in the production process was the subject of an independent choice-of-technology decision. In the final stage of equipment selection, however, efforts were sometimes made to introduce some uniformity among these decisions. In the acquisition of cotton manufacturing equipment, such uniformity was found to be sought in the selection of equipment manufacturers, particularly for the opening room and for the spinning shed. Although it is often felt that the use of equipment from different manufacturers in each step of production—even in such a continuous operation as the opening room—does not pose any significant technical problems, textile companies generally preferred to limit the total number of their equipment suppliers.

They believed that larger orders might result in better financial conditions from the supplier, might secure better after-sales service, and might facilitate maintenance and reduce spare parts inventories, the result of the tendency of manufacturers to standardize simple parts used in their entire line of machinery. In plant expansions the same factors were found to have argued for the selection of the equipment manufacturers that had supplied the original equipment.

Overall, however, efforts to reduce the number of equipment suppliers did not seem to have played an important role in the final choice of equipment. Most of the production facilities visited included equipment from a large variety of equipment suppliers. This was even the case in a single processing step among plants that had gone through several capacity expansions. Furthermore such factors should not have had much impact on the choice of technology since most equipment suppliers produce models that embody several technologies and offer equipment for several consecutive processing steps.

Availability of Information

Along with the cost of the factors of production, the prime factor that was found to have influenced the choice of technology by the firms in this study was the lack of information about certain existing technological alternatives. Because of this lack of information, equipment embodying these technological alternatives was never included in the list of alternatives submitted by engineers at the first stage of the decision process. Consequently these alternatives were never evaluated. These omissions introduced a definite bias into the ultimate choice since the technologies for which information was not available tended to be the more labor-intensive ones.

Information Flows and Capital Intensity

Information and technological knowledge tend to follow the flow of trade. As a consequence such information and knowledge are exchanged more commonly between developed and developing countries than among developing countries. Virtually all of the information available in developing countries about existing technological alternatives and equipment manufacturers was found to have originated in developed countries. At the same time equipment manufacturers from developed countries tend to respond to the signals they receive from their immediate environment and to the needs of their largest customers, also from developed countries. For that reason these equipment manufacturers usually tend to develop their product range at the capital-intensive end of the spectrum and, conversely, will tend to drop technological alternatives considered too labor intensive for their key customers. Thus the equipment they develop and promote is characterized by high investment cost, high operating speed, and a high degree of automation. Small amounts of unskilled and semiskilled labor are typically required to operate these machines and perform handling tasks, while relatively large amounts of skilled maintenance work are needed to keep them in condition for top efficiency operation.

In this already restricted group of equipment manufacturers whose products are known in developing countries, those that will receive the greatest amount of publicity and attention from the professional media will be the most innovative ones. Expert reviews, professional meetings, and equipment fairs tend to emphasize what is new. Engineers from developing countries who obtain a large part of their product information from these professional media (as opposed to personal contacts) will therefore tend to receive the bulk of their product information about the newest and generally most capital-intensive segment of the product range. Since they are in a less price-competitive segment of the equipment market, the most innovative equipment manufacturers will also be those that can spend the largest amounts on marketing and sales promotion. Clearly this will reinforce the tendency toward easier availability of information about the most capital-intensive technology alternatives.

Equipment manufacturers headquartered in developing countries, on the other hand, were found to offer more labor-intensive equipment. Already constrained in their capacity to develop new models by the scarcity of research personnel, they also did not face a demand for capital-intensive machinery in their domestic market. Because of the patterns followed by information flows, however, these equipment suppliers were found to be unknown to engineers in other developing countries. Because the equipment they offer is based on long-recognized technologies, it did not receive attention in professional publications. Furthermore since they served a primarily local market, these manufacturers were also smaller and lacked the financial capacity to send sales personnel to international equipment fairs or to maintain representatives abroad and engage in sales promotion.

Developing Countries as Sources of Adapted Technologies

The survey of textile equipment manufacturers on which this study is based and the lists of alternatives considered by the firms investigated clearly confirm the patterns just described. Table 4.1 shows whether each technological alternative in this study was found in equipment manufactured in developed countries or in developing countries. For equipment manufactured in developing countries, a distinction has been made as to whether it was produced under license from developed countries' firms or from local designs. It appears from this table that some of the most labor-intensive technologies are produced only in developing countries from local designs. (Some of these local designs are in fact copies of equipment originally manufactured in developed countries; however, such designs are now so common that developed countries' firms do not claim rights to them anymore.)

Another group of labor-intensive technologies is manufactured in developed countries as well as in developing countries, customarily under license. This is generally equipment whose production is in the process of being slowly phased out in the developed countries and for which equipment manufacturers from these countries are ready to grant licenses. Finally the more capital-intensive technologies were found to be available only from developed countries.

It has often been argued that the technologies available only from suppliers in developing countries are not relevant to the choice because of a lack of efficiency. This is not so, as the last column of table 4.1 shows. In fact these technologies constituted the social optimum in both the carding and the weaving steps in all of the countries studied. In addition they represented the market optimum in 24 of the 110 cases of technology choice studied.

Only two developing countries—India and Korea—produce textile equipment embodying technologies not available from developed countries' equipment manufacturers in any significant quantities.[4] Colombia produces only one model of loom of a technology that is also available from developed countries. Indonesia and the Philippines do

Table 4.1
Place of Manufacture and Competitiveness of Alternative Technologies

Processing Step	Alternative Technology	Place of Manufacture			Social Optimum Technology					Number of Cases in Developing Countries in which that Alternative was	
		Developed Countries	Developing Countries		Colombia	Brazil (south)	Brazil (northeast)	Philippines	Indonesia	Market Optimum	Chosen
			Under License	Local Design							
Plucking	Alternative 1	X	X	X	X	X	X	X	X	10	14
	Alternative 2	X								6	0
	Alternative 3	X								0	2
Scutching	Alternative 1	X	X		X	X	X	X	X	13	7
	Alternative 2	X	X							0	3
	Alternative 3	X								0	2
	Alternative 4	X								0	0
	Alternative 5	X	Planned							3	4
Carding	Alternative 1	Discontinued		X						0	3
	Alternative 2	Discontinued	X		X	X	X	X	X	16	2
	Alternative 3	X	Planned							0	5
	Alternative 4	X	Planned							0	2

Alternative 5	X							0	3
Alternative 6	X							0	1
Alternative 7	X							0	0
Drawing									
Alternative 1	X	X		X		X	X	4	5
Alternative 2	X				X			12	9
Alternative 3	X							0	2
Alternative 4	X							0	0
Winding									
Alternative 1	X	X	X	X	X	X	X	7	8
Alternative 2	X	Planned						6	2
Alternative 3	X							3	4
Alternative 4	X							0	2
Alternative 5	X							0	0
Alternative 6	X							0	0
Alternative 7	X							0	0
Alternative 8	X							0	0
Pirn winding									
Alternative 1	X		X			X	X	0	0
Alternative 2	X	X		X	X			10	9
Alternative 3	X							5	4
Alternative 4	X							0	2
Weaving									
Alternative 1	X		X			X	X	0	0
Alternative 2			X					0	0
Alternative 3			X	X	X			8	0
Alternative 4	X	X	X					7	4
Alternative 5	X	X						0	8

Table 4.1
Place of Manufacture and Competitiveness of Alternative Technologies

Processing Step	Alternative Technology	Place of Manufacture			Social Optimum Technology					Number of Cases in Developing Countries in which that Alternative was	
		Developed Countries	Developing Countries		Colombia	Brazil (south)	Brazil (northeast)	Philippines	Indonesia	Market Optimum	Chosen
			Under License	Local Design							
	Alternative 6	X								0	2
	Alternative 7	X								0	1
	Alternative 8	X								0	0
	Alternative 9	X								0	0
	Alternative 10	X								0	0

not produce any textile equipment apart from hand looms. For the processing steps analyzed in this study, even Brazil produces only equipment that is similar in design to machinery produced by developed countries and does so only under license from firms in these countries. Therefore for none of the textile firms studied, with the only exception of the Indonesian subsidiary of an Indian firm, were these labor-intensive technologies (which are offered only by developing countries' equipment manufacturers) domestic alternatives.

While the most labor-intensive technologies were available only from developing countries, none of the firms studied, with the exception of the Indian venture in Indonesia, chose equipment from these countries. Pointing even more clearly to this information gap is the fact that such equipment was not included in any of the lists of available alternatives considered by the firms studied. When asked about these omissions, the engineers responsible for drawing up these lists generally answered that they had heard about textile equipment produced in developing countries but were unacquainted with the names of the manufacturers or the types of equipment they offered. They often added that although they had no precise information, they had heard or were under the impression that this equipment was not of good quality or was inefficient.

The result of this lack of information was that the technologies chosen were often the most labor-intensive ones available from developed countries, although still suboptimal in comparison with technologies available from other developing countries.

Risk-Minimization Considerations

Risk-minimizing considerations enter into the firm's technology choices in three different ways. First, the pricing of the equity, and of the loans used by a firm to finance a new project, incorporates an evaluation of the political and business risk faced by the venture. Second, the use of each factor of production, equipment or labor, carries not only a cost but also a risk that this factor will not operate at the expected standards. The exact form and extent of this risk is dependent upon the nature of the factor. Third, when choosing a technology, a firm may not only be expected to attempt to maximize its anticipated profits but may also be expected to reduce the variability of these profits by stabilizing its competitive position vis-à-vis other firms in the industry.

Business and Political Risk

The firm's cost of capital used in the computation of transformation costs includes the evaluation of political and business risk by the suppliers of capital. Therefore these risks have already been accounted for in the determination of the market optimum technology. One would expect that business and political risks would not further influence the choice-of-technology decision. The suppliers of funds to the firm should be willing to provide any reasonable amount required to finance projects with an expected rate of return on investment at least equal to the cost of capital.

Yet even after they adjusted their cost of capital according to the business and political risks involved in financing projects in developing countries, executives of developed countries' firms stressed that minimization of the investment cost of the project in developing countries was an important consideration in their choice of technology. On the other hand this factor was not perceived as being important by local firms or firms from other developing countries. All other things equal, one might therefore expect subsidiaries of developed countries' firms to choose more labor-intensive technologies than local firms or subsidiaries of developing countries' firms.

Risk Associated with Factors of Production

In discussions with the managers of textile firms in developing countries, the concept of risk associated with the use of different factors of production emerged as a powerful notion, although the executives seldom conceptualized these risks in such a manner. The risk associated with the use of capital goods stems from the uncertain availability of spare parts and of outside technical assistance in the event of a major technical problem. This risk becomes significant in developing countries because of their distance from equipment manufacturers, the difficulty of communication, and the unavailability of services such as machine shops and engineering and consulting firms. These and other local conditions, including frequent delays in shipping and granting of foreign exchange and import licenses for spare parts, make the operation of equipment in developing countries much more problematic than in developed countries. The potential for serious production problems increases with the degree of sophistication and automation of the equipment. To minimize this risk, firms in developing countries generally limit themselves to conventional equipment of proven and well-known design and to equipment manufactured by large firms with an international service network.

Associated with the use of labor are the risks of strikes or labor unrest and of human error in the operation of the machines. These risks would normally induce management to try to minimize the overall number of workers by automating the production facilities. Training of workers cannot altogether eliminate human error. For the firm these risks can translate into costs in terms of decreased machine efficiency, loss of raw material, reduction in quality, or even damage to the equipment.

Impact on Technology Choice
The risk associated with the use of capital and the risk associated with the use of labor tend to pull the choice-of-technology decision of a firm in opposite directions. Capital risk justifies the adoption of technologies that are more labor intensive than the market optimum. Labor risk justifies the adoption of technologies that are more capital intensive than the optimum. These two forms of risk, however, can be expected to exert varied influences on the different aspects of the choice-of-technology decisions that firms make. They are also given different weights depending upon the characteristics of the firm and on the production step for which a technology is being chosen.

The risk associated with the use of capital influences the choice of an equipment manufacturer as much as, if not more than, the choice of a technology. Firms in developing countries were found to be all the more sensitive to this risk when they selected equipment for operations that could be performed manually without negative impact on the product's quality or uniformity.

As to risks associated with labor, firms appear to assume that the likelihood of labor unrest increases in a more than proportional manner with the size of the labor force employed. Such an assumption should lead these organizations to the conclusion that the larger the production facility, the more the need to automate. Foreign-owned firms are also more sensitive to these risks and therefore more inclined to automate their plants because of the frequent difficulties and uneasiness on the part of headquarter and expatriate managers in dealing with indigenous workers. An association with strong local partners should, however, reduce this tendency toward automation. Generally local partners take charge of worker relations, thus relieving the foreign enterprise of this delicate problem.

Costs associated with human error vary widely according to the industry, the step in the process in which the error occurs, and the type of task to be performed manually. The cost of a human error is higher in processing steps that are critical to the end product's quality or in steps in which a small number of processing units transform all of the plant's output. Consequently the propensity of companies to automate these steps is higher than for other less crucial ones. At the same time the cost of human error is low in material handling operations, whether they are between-step material transfers or loading, unloading, and waste collection operations within a processing step. For this reason, as well as due to their search for simpler, more conventional machines, firms are less ready to automate these steps and operations through the adoption of automatic transfer equipment or automatic loading and unloading features for their machines.

Technology Choices Made
The firms studied were guided by risk considerations in choosing more automated and capital-intensive technologies for the crucial steps in the production process than for the less critical ones. In a given processing step they also seem more prone to adopt automated features in order to replace manpower in quality-related operations even if the manual options are economically justified. Three steps of the seven examined in the analysis of textile production were classified as crucial: scutching, carding, and weaving. In the carding and weaving steps operations are performed that are crucial to the quality of the end product. The scutching step is critical because a few units of machinery process the output of the entire plant.

Of the forty-seven choices of technology involving steps that were considered critical, thirty-four were for technologies that were more capital-intensive than the market optimum. Only thirteen were for the market optimum or a technology even more labor intensive. In non-critical steps these proportions are reversed: in only sixteen of the sixty-three cases was the chosen technology more capital intensive than the market optimum. In the other forty-seven cases the market optimum or an even more labor-intensive technology was chosen. A comparison of the propensities to adapt exhibited by the firms for these two groups of processing steps yields the same results: average propensities to adapt turned out to be eighty-one for critical steps and fifty-seven for noncritical steps.

It was also found that in any one processing step, capital-intensive technologies consisting of improvements in the transformation operations were considered and adopted more often than capital-intensive technologies based on the automation of materials handling. In other words the automation of tasks that change the nature of the material were adopted more often than the automatic feeding or unloading of this material—this even though the latter were more justified from the economic point of view. Direct on-the-loom pirn winding (Unifil system) was considered and adopted more often than automatic feeding on conventional pirn winding frames. Similarly chute feeding of cards was considered more often than automatic handling added to scutchers, and high-speed cards and draw frames were adopted more often than automatic doffing on lower-speed cards and draw frames.

Confirmation of this was also found in the rules of thumb used by some firms in making technology choices. When planning investments in developing countries, the parent firm of one of the facilities studied as a rule only adopts equipment stripped of all automatic features that are not directly linked with the transformation or quality stabilization of the end product. Automatic feeding, unloading, automatic transport, and automatic waste collection features are therefore systematically excluded.

While the critical nature of the processing step and of the operation to be performed were found to condition choices of technology, plant size was not found to be a factor in technology choice. None of the measures of size of the production facility were found to be significantly related to the firm's propensity to adapt. It should be remembered, however, that all of the production facilities studied processed at least one thousand pounds of fiber per hour, an already large volume of production and one beyond which economies of scale are considered to play an important role.

Similarly no significant difference was found between the choice of technology of foreign-owned firms and locally owned firms. In 50 percent of their technology choices foreign-owned firms chose a technology at the market optimum or that was more labor intensive than the market optimum. Locally owned firms did so in 57 percent of their choices. Supporting this finding, the average propensity to adapt of foreign-owned firms was 67 percent against 77 percent for locally owned firms. (See table 4.2.) The direction of this small difference in degree of labor intensity is in fact reversed when the data are adjusted to eliminate differences between these two groups of firms in the extent

Table 4.2
Ownership, Product Differentiation, and Choice of Technology

	Majority Locally Owned			Majority Foreign Owned	Total
	Private	Government	Total		
Nonproduct differentiating					
Number of companies	7	2	9	3 (0)	12
% of choices at market optimum or more labor intensive	61	29	54	67	57
Average propensity to adapt	81	54	75	89	79
Product differentiating					
Number of companies	1	0	1	3 (3)	4
% of choices at market optimum or more labor intensive	86		86	32	46
Average propensity to adapt	89		89	45	56
Total					
Number of companies	8	2	10	6 (3)	16
% of choices at market optimum or more labor intensive	64	29	57	50	55
Average propensity to adapt	82	51	77	67	73

Note: Only facilities located in developing countries are included in this table. The home country facilities of the developed countries firms are therefore excluded.
a. In parentheses are shown the number of foreign companies that were majority owned by other developing country firms.

of public ownership and product differentiation strategies, factors that were found to influence technology choice. Private, locally owned, nonproduct differentiating firms chose the market optimum or a more labor-intensive technology in 61 percent of their choices and had an average propensity to adapt of 81. For private, foreign-owned, nonproduct differentiating firms, the figures were 67 percent and 89, respectively. These figures are more meaningful than the preceding ones since the proportions of government-owned firms and firms with a strategy of product differentiation in these subsamples were not meant to be representative of the world or the countries from which the sample was drawn.

The fact that foreign and local firms did not differ significantly in their choices of technology does not mean, however, that they made similar evaluations of the risk factors. Identical choices of technology might have been the result of mutually offsetting influences. Evidence of this was found in the fact that foreign firms showed a higher sensitivity to both political risk and risk of labor unrest than did local firms. While sensitivity to political risk should have resulted in a minimization of investment cost and therefore a preference for labor-intensive technologies, sensitivity to risk of labor unrest should have dictated a reduction in the size of the labor force and therefore a tendency to favor capital-intensive alternatives. Taken together these two factors seem to have resulted in similar choices of technologies for both foreign and local firms.

The task of evaluating the impact on the choice of a manufacturer of these risk factors, particularly the risk associated with the use of capital, requires dealing with very subjective judgments such as reputations and perceived reliability. Furthermore managers can easily use such judgments for self-justification. In some instances, however, such risk considerations clearly influenced the choice of equipment manufacturer although a spectrum of alternative technologies was still available from each of the manufacturers considered. For example, when one firm expanded capacity, it purchased looms of the same technology, design, and price as those already installed but from a different manufacturer. According to the firm's managers the only reason was that the original supplier's share of the international market had declined, and they were afraid that this would lead to a scaling down of its international representation and after-sale service network.

Risk Associated with Deviations from Leader's Choice

Studies of the patterns of decision making in areas other than technology choice, such as studies of the foreign investment decision, have demonstrated the importance of "follow the leader" behavior.[5] If such behavior exists in technology choice, smaller firms would choose the same technologies and the same equipment manufacturers as the industry leaders in that market. By doing so, the smaller firms would minimize the risk of finding themselves priced out of the market because the equipment they chose failed to operate according to expectations or because of changes in the relative cost of the factors of production.

The managers of relatively small, locally owned firms often noted that the choice of equipment made by the larger firms in the industry had a major influence on their choices. Conversely among foreign-owned firms, it was not the equipment choices made by industry leaders in the host country but rather the choices made in home country plants that were deemed important. In both cases, however, these considerations were seen as having influenced the choice of a manufacturer rather than the choice of a technology. Comparisons of the technology choices made pointed to a great deal of similarity in the choice of equipment manufacturers made by industry leaders and by smaller local manufacturers in a country as well as by headquarters and their subsidiaries. On the other hand a large variance was found in the technologies chosen by these different firms.

The reason offered by smaller local firms for their choice of the same equipment manufacturers as those chosen by the industry leaders was that the large orders these manufacturers had received from industry leaders had caused them to develop a local after-sales service capacity and to schedule regular servicing visits to the country. The reason why subsidiaries of multinational firms chose the same equipment sources as their headquarters facilities was quite similar. In their case, however, it was the size of the home country orders that were motivating the equipment suppliers to develop adequate service facilities in the country where the subsidiary was located. Smaller local firms as well as subsidiaries of foreign firms did not consider it important to adopt the same technologies as the industry leaders or the home country facilities. They considered textile technologies, even the newer ones, to be relatively simple and to have been thoroughly tested. This gave them a high degree of confidence in their capacity to evaluate these technologies.

Competitive Pressure on the Firm

One of the first studies of the technology choices made by subsidiaries of multinational firms concluded that competitive pressure was one of the main determinants of the degree to which these firms adapted to the relative prices of the factors of production in the host country.[6] This study found that subsidiaries of U.S. firms whose market position was highly dependent on price competitiveness were more likely to adopt labor-intensive technologies than were subsidiaries of U.S. firms that managed to escape such competitive pressure. In the absence of competitive pressure considerations other than production cost minimization dictated the technology choice decision. One such consideration might be a concentration on technological features that would further the firm's capacity to differentiate its products on the basis of quality for example. Another might be a minimization of risk regardless of the associated costs, such as by minimizing the risk of labor unrest through reductions in labor force. Concentration on savings of one of the factors of production might be yet another consideration, such as savings of management time through the choice of familiar technologies.

Firms might escape competitive pressures for three reasons:

1. They might have a monopoly or oligopoly position.

2. Although in a basically competitive market, they might have been allocated a share of that market through automatic subsidies.

3. They might have a strategy of product differentiation that positions them out of price-competitive segments of the market.

Although the import of ordinary short-fiber cloth was banned in all the countries studied, there were enough domestic producers so that none of them could be considered to have a monopoly or oligopoly position. Government-owned or cooperatively owned firms, on the other hand, were guaranteed a market whatever their production cost, within reasonable limits. They should therefore be considered as having been shielded from competitive pressure. Product-differentiation strategies can be identified by an objective criterion such as the price premium the products of a firm commanded in the market or by a relatively subjective criterion such as management's reply to a question designed to elicit whether the firm had a strategy of product differentiation. A subjective criterion was used for this study since the choice-of-technology decisions made by the firm will depend on its intended strategy rather than on how successful the implementation of that strategy had actually been.

Table 4.2 presents the percentage of technology choices where the market optimum or a technology more labor intensive than that market optimum was chosen by type of firm ownership and product strategy as well as the average propensity to adapt exhibited by firms in each of these categories.

These figures show that government-owned firms and firms with a strategy of product differentiation made choices of technology that were significantly different from those of other firms. Government-owned firms did not view themselves as having a strategy of product differentiation; however, they clearly chose technologies that were much more capital intensive in relation to their market optimum than did nonproduct-differentiating, privately owned local firms. In only 29 percent of their choices did government-owned firms choose a technology that was either cost minimizing or more labor intensive than this optimum. The corresponding figure for privately owned, nonproduct-differentiating firms was 61 percent. Government-owned firms exhibited an average propensity to adapt of 54, as opposed to 81 for their private counterparts. Furthermore this lesser propensity to adapt cannot be attributed to a lower cost of capital since the determination of the market optimum technology for these government-owned firms already took into account their lower cost of capital. (In determining the market optimum, the cost of the equity part of the capital of government-owned firms was considered to be zero since this equity was provided in the form of government grants for which the government required no income.) As a consequence the market optimum for government-owned firms was already more capital intensive than the optimum for private firms.

The lower propensity to adapt of government-owned firms is explained by the fact that their sales, within reasonable limits, were insensitive to production costs. They were assured of selling all of their output either in captive markets (government purchases, cooperatives contracts) or with the help of government subsidies. Cost minimization therefore played a very limited role, if any, in their choice of technology. At the same time criteria of engineering excellence and risk minimization exerted the heaviest influence on their decisions. In fact the firms classified as public enterprises in this study were managed by engineers with limited business experience. As far as could be determined, technology choices were made on technical rather than economic grounds.[7]

Of the four firms that had a strategy of product differentiation, three were majority foreign owned and one was of purely local ownership. The three foreign firms considered quality to be the basic characteristic by which they differentiated their output from that of other firms. These three firms made technology choices significantly more capital intensive than did the other foreign-owned firms. They chose the market optimum technology or technologies more labor intensive than the market optimum in 32 percent of their decisions versus 67 percent for the other foreign firms. Their propensity to adapt was 45 against 89 for the other foreign firms.

The locally owned firm with a strategy of product differentiation specialized in the production of small orders on short notice. This firm was also found to have had a different pattern of technology choices from other private, locally owned firms. In this case though, the technologies it chose were more labor intensive than those chosen by the other firms. This firm chose the cost-minimizing technology, or a technology even more labor intensive, in 86 percent of the cases, and it exhibited a propensity to adapt of 89 as against 61 percent and 81, respectively, in the cases of private, locally owned, nonproduct-differentiating firms. In fact, in 57 percent of the cases, the technology this firm chose was even more labor intensive than the cost-minimizing technology. In the words of its manager, the choice of labor-intensive machinery resulted in a "high flexibility of production, since each unit has a small production capacity." Besides its policy of choosing labor-intensive equipment when purchasing new equipment, this firm also had a policy of buying second-hand equipment whenever possible and maintaining it as reserve production capacity.

The three foreign-owned firms that had a strategy of product differentiation were the only ones in the sample that were owned by a parent from another developing country. Despite the small size of this group, the high correlation between product-differentiating strategy based on quality and inter-developing-country ownership manifested here is intriguing. This link is all the more surprising since product differentiation based on quality was found to be associated with a higher level of capital intensity. Inter-developing-countries' investment has generally been assumed to lead to the adoption of more labor-intensive technologies than did investment of developed countries' firms. Developing countries' firms have been thought to select technologies more adapted to other developing countries than developed countries' firms because of the similarities in their home and host environments. This hypothesis should have been particularly true in the cases studied here since the home and host environments of these developing countries' firms were very similar in terms of size and cost of the factors of production.

Due to the small sample size, only a tentative explanation of this phenomenon can be offered, but a look at the parent firms of these inter-developing-countries' ventures may offer a logical explanation for this unexpected finding. As was the case here, the developing country firms that invest in other developing countries are characteristically the most successful and modern ones in their home country. These companies tend to be managed by people trained in developed countries. They have built their success upon the application of Western management concepts such as product differentiation, marketing intensity, and diversification strategies. In their home country, where wages are also relatively low, they stressed product quality and brand image rather than low-cost production. It was found that their decision to invest abroad was part of a strategy of geographical diversification and a search for a similar market in which to apply the formulas that brought them success at home. It was not motivated by the availability of cheap labor and the potential for low-cost production. Developed countries' firms, on the other hand, having been accustomed to high wage structures, appeared to be much more sensitive to lower labor costs and more inclined to take advantage of such differences. They also considered the availability of low-cost labor to be the main reason for their decision to invest in developing countries.

Government Non-Factor-Price Policies

In determining market optimum technologies, all government policies that affect the relative market prices of the factors of production were taken into account. Other policies, however, influence technology choice without changing the market price of the factors of production. Since the impact of such policies was not taken into account in the determination of the market optimum, their effect should be reflected in the gap between market optimum and technology chosen.

A wide variety of government non-factor-price policies affect the technology-choice decision. An example of such policies is the arbitrary allocation of foreign exchange and credit when market prices of these factors have not been allowed to assume levels that balance demand and supply. Another example is the granting of tax rebates and tax holidays, which indirectly influence the cost of capital to the firm. Two sets of government policies were found to have influenced the choice of technology of the firms studied: government policies dealing with the origin and the financing of equipment purchases and tax credits and concessions offered by governments to promote investments of specific characteristics.

Government Policies Dealing with Local Production and Import of Machinery

These policies were found to narrow the range of alternatives available to decision makers and to do so mostly at the expense of the more labor-intensive technologies.

In developing countries that do not have a domestic production of textile equipment, the government policy often is to allow capital goods imports only if they are financed by foreign credits of a minimum length of time. Such a policy leads to the de facto exclusion of smaller machinery producers, which lack the financial capacity to extend such credit, and of producers from other developing countries that are not backed by a government-sponsored export financing organization. Such a situation was found in a more or less acute manner in Colombia, Indonesia, and the Philippines.

These policies took a different form in Brazil since this country has a textile equipment industry. To promote the development of its domestic capital goods industry, the government of Brazil had put a de facto ban on the import of any equipment that is or can be produced in the country. The locally owned companies that produce equipment, however, are generally not specialized, and because of lack of experience encounter difficulties in adhering to specifications and delivery dates. At least this is how prospective purchasers of equipment viewed them. To avoid having to order from them, equipment purchasers often selected machinery of a degree of sophistication high enough for an import authorization to be granted on the grounds that such equipment could not be manufactured locally.

When, on the other hand, the domestic equipment producer is the subsidiary of a foreign firm, for financial reasons it is most likely to be the subsidiary of one of the large developed countries' machinery producers. These companies tend to build their comparative advantage through innovation in the most sophisticated, most automated end of the technology spectrum. Furthermore because of the limited size of the internal market, only one such company typically seeks to produce locally any one type of capital goods. Even if several applications for domestic production are made, only one will normally be approved. Not having any competitive pressure from other domestic producers or from imports, this machinery producer has no incentive to adapt its models to local market conditions. In fact it has every incentive to produce the same models as in its home country in order to spread its research and development costs and sell equipment of a high unit price. The result is that such equipment manufacturers tend to produce equipment that is much more capital intensive than justified by local conditions.

The impact of these policies was apparent in specific technology choices of the Brazilian firms studied and was confirmed in discussions with the management of these firms. These policies, however, did not play a role in the choice of technology for processing steps studied earlier because no significant amount of equipment was domestically produced for these production steps.

Tax Credits and Fiscal Incentives

To encourage the localization of industrial ventures in northeast Brazil, the government has been offering important incentives to firms relocating part of their operations in this underdeveloped part of the country. These incentives mostly take the form of tax credits granted to the parent company. These credits were to be equal to a certain percentage of the capital cost of the facilities built in the northeast. Yet several studies have already indicated that although the objective of this policy is to create employment in this region, the form of the incentives granted actually encouraged capital intensity.[8] The evidence collected in this study, although of a limited scope, seems to be in line with the conclusions of these previous studies. Of the two Brazilian textile production facilities studied, one was located in the region of São Paulo and the other in northeast Brazil. They belonged to the same industrial group, were constructed at about the same time, and produced relatively similar goods. Because of the lower cost of labor in northeast Brazil, the market optimum technologies in this region were found to be more labor intensive than in the region of São Paulo. Since all other factors considered to influence technology choice were identical, it might be expected that the technologies chosen for the northeast facility would also be more labor intensive. Instead the technologies chosen were found to be more capital intensive than those chosen for the São Paulo region, and the propensity to adapt shown in planning the northeast facility was markedly lower than in the São Paulo facility. Because the only factors that changed between these two production facilities were the fiscal incentives granted, this difference in behavior can be attributed only to the impact of these incentives.

Fiscal incentives such as tax holidays and carrying forward of losses for tax purposes that were granted to firms in other countries also played a role in the choices of technology that were made, although in a less dramatic manner. These incentives seem to be the reason why firms in Indonesia had a lower average propensity to adapt than firms in Colombia and the Philippines. In Indonesia such incentives are granted quite liberally, while Colombia and the Philippines put much more serious restrictions on their allocation. If fiscal incentives granted by a country have in fact influenced the general technology profile of the firms studied, such a finding would contradict statements made by the management of these firms that tax considerations did not play a role in their choice of production technologies.

5

**The Pulp and
Paper Industry:
Dimensions of
Production Cost
Minimization**

The pulp and paper industry differs from the textile industry in a number of fundamental ways that bear on the scope, form, and implications of technology choice. These differences make it impossible to isolate and measure the impact of factor prices on technology choice in the pulp and paper industry in the same way as was done for the textile industry. Although much can be learned from a comparison of technology choice between these two industries, one needs to go a step further and develop a new framework for the analysis of technology choices in chemical process industries.

Differences between the Characteristics of the Textile and Pulp and Paper Industries

Economies of Scale

Economies of scale in the pulp and paper industry are much more important than in the textile industry. To take advantage of them, pulp and paper companies need to build extremely large mills that require more sophisticated technologies and larger markets than in the textile industry.

Figures 5.1 and 5.2 chart the economies of scale of pulp mills and of integrated pulp and paper mills, respectively. An 800-ton-per-day integrated sulfate pulp and paper mill requires half of the investment per ton capacity that a 170-ton-per-day mill would require. Even for a 400-ton-per-day mill—a capacity considered to represent the minimum economic size in the industry—a 20 percent increase in planned capacity would only result in a 10 percent increase in investment cost.

The problem posed by the importance of economies of scale in the pulp and paper industry is compounded by the fact that a mill of

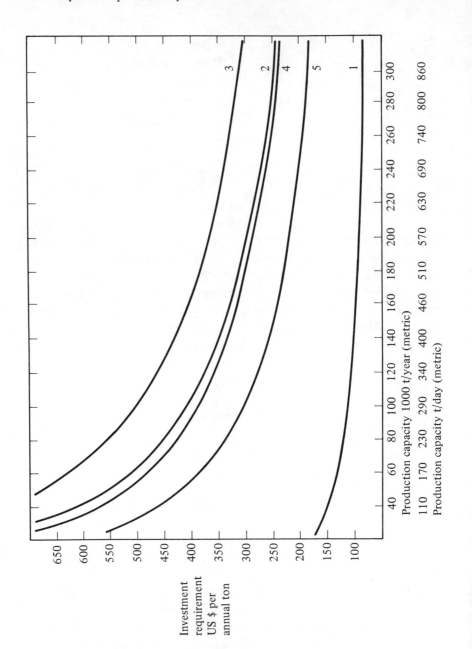

Figure 5.1
Investment Requirements for Pulp Mills as Function of Mill Size
Approximate coefficients for different countries (difference in output excluded):

Sweden   1.0
US South States 1.05
British Columbia 1.15
Brazil   1.10
Finland   0.95

Local conditions and the extension of project result in variation of $+10\% \ldots -30\%$

Cost level: Costs are for mills started during 1972.

The investment is total mill capital including general costs and auxiliary departments, but excluding interest during construction period and working capital.

1. Groundwood (spruce) AD-pulp
2. Unbleached sulfate (pine) AD-pulp
3. Bleached sulfate (pine) AD-pulp
4. Bleached magnefite (spruce) AD-pulp
5. Unbleached magnefite (spruce) AD-pulp

Source: Jaakko Poyry & Co., Consulting Engineers.

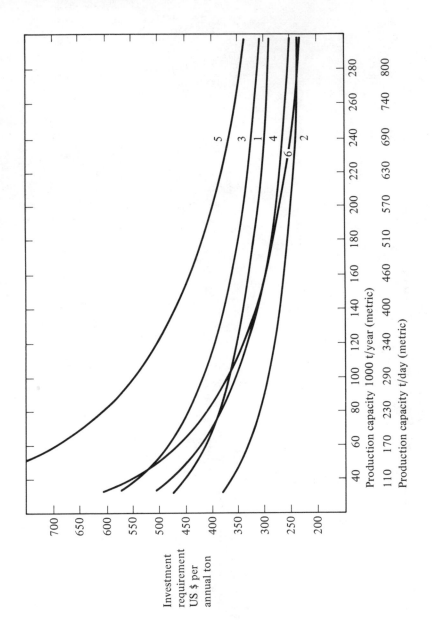

Figure 5.2
Investment Requirements for Paper and Board Mills as Function of Mill Size

Approximate coefficients for different countries (differences in output excluded):

Sweden	1.0
US South States	1.105
British Columbia	1.15
Brazil	1.10
Finland	0.95

Local conditions and the extension of project result in variation of +10% . . . −30%.

Cost level: Costs are for mills started during 1972.

The investment is total mill capital including general costs and auxiliary departments, but excluding interest during construction period and working capital.

1. Newsprint mill, integrated with groundwood mill
2. Newsprint mill, non-integrated
3. Mechanical printing paper mill, integrated with groundwood mill
4. Mechanical printing paper mill, non-integrated
5. Kraftliner mill, integrated with sulfate pulp mill (high yield—normal pulp)
6. Fluting board (corrugating medium) mill, integrated with NSSC pulp mill, with recovery

Source: Jaakko Poyry & Co., Consulting Engineers.

minimum economic size in that industry requires a very large market to be able to operate at capacity. The output of a 15,000-spindle textile mill represents the average textile fiber consumption of about 1 million people in developing countries. The output of a 400-ton-per-day pulp and paper mill, on the other hand, represents the consumption of all types of paper, from newsprint to cardboard, of about 35 million people at the average level of per-capita consumption that prevails in developing countries.

Because of this difference in minimum economic scale of production, textile mills in developing countries are much more common and generally operate at a much more efficient scale than do pulp and paper mills. While practically all developing countries have at least one textile mill and most have several, very few have even a single pulp and paper mill. Furthermore while all textile mills in developing countries are larger than the minimum economic size, pulp and paper mills in these countries rarely approach the minimum economic scale of production. Developing countries produce nearly half of the world's textiles but only 5 percent of the world's pulp and 7 percent of the world's paper.[1] The entire pulp production of developing countries is equivalent only to the output of fifty-five mills of minimum economic size.

The limited scope of the pulp and paper industry in developing countries was evident in the countries examined. Colombia has only three wood pulp mills (including one of 50-ton-per-day capacity), the Philippines has only three (including two of 50-ton-per-day capacity), and Indonesia has five pulp mills, all with less than 50-ton-per-day capacity. Among the countries investigated only Brazil has a sizable pulp and paper industry. Its daily pulping capacity was 3,600 tons in the mid-1970s and was distributed among some forty-two pulp mills, of which nine had a capacity of more than 100 tons per day. Several large pulp mills (above 800-ton-per-day capacity) were also being planned or under construction at that time.

Custom-Made Equipment

The pulp and paper industry's technology is neither standardized nor widely known, and the equipment it uses is generally custom made.

It is true that general principles of chemical pulping through the sulfate process and of bleaching and papermaking are widely known; however, the adaptation of these general principles to the pulping and bleaching of a specific type of wood or to the production of a specific type of paper is usually unique to each production facility. Although there is some amount of consistency within certain species, the wood used as raw material by each facility has its own set of characteristics, depending not only upon its species but also upon soil and weather conditions. What is often called the art of pulp and papermaking consists of finding the combination of chemicals, temperature, pressure, and time that will transform this wood into a pulp of given characteristics and then defining the mix of different pulps that will yield a paper that satisfies specific requirements.

Each time a new facility is planned, a relatively fresh start in technology must be undertaken. It must take advantage of the experience accumulated by the firm or the hired consultants and take into consideration not only the characteristics of the wood to be used but also the availability and cost of various processing chemicals. This effort will lead to an original definition of the characteristics and design of the equipment that should be used.

This is in sharp contrast to the textile industry with its high degree of standardization of both inputs and output, as well as the small size of the basic unit of production in each of its processing steps. At the same time the large number of textile manufacturing facilities that are started each year makes it feasible for equipment manufacturers to standardize their production and offer off-the-shelf pieces of equipment. Such standardization does not exist in the pulp and paper industry where the main pieces of equipment must be built to order. According to a survey of 1975 by the Food and Agriculture Organization, the additional yearly capacity of wood pulping to be built during the five year period 1975–1979 was expected to be 27.5 million tons. If, following historical patterns, it is assumed that half of this additional capacity will use chemical pulping processes, only 7,800 daily tons of capacity of chemical pulp will be installed in an average year. This would correspond to an equivalent of twelve 600-ton-per-day projects being started each year. The major pieces of equipment (digesters, recovery furnaces, bleaching towers, evaporation towers, and paper machines) would have to be designed specifically for each project, and in most of these projects only a single unit of each item of equipment will be installed.

Sources of Information

Most of the analysis and design work required for a project in the pulp and paper industry is generally contracted to outside organizations.

Even the largest and most experienced manufacturers do so, in contrast with the textile industry where most, if not all, of this work is done inside the firm. Furthermore the number of organizations such as consulting firms and equipment manufacturers that are capable of undertaking such a design effort for a new mill is surprisingly small. Only five or six large multidisciplinary consulting firms in the world specialize in forest-related industries and are large enough to undertake the planning and coordinate the construction of a new mill. For each of the main processing steps, only between four and ten equipment manufacturers in the entire world are original sources of technology. Some of these, however, might license other suppliers to produce equipment based on their designs.

Since these few consultants and equipment manufacturers act as pools of information for the industry and participate in the design of all important projects, a large degree of uniformity of concepts exists within the industry. In fact the characteristics of a mill and the choices of technology that are made for it appear to have more to do with the firm that acted as general consultant than with the ownership of the mill—be it public or private, local or foreign.

None of the general pulp and paper design and consulting firms has its headquarters in developing countries, although a few have opened offices in Brazil. Only one manufacturer of specialized equipment for the pulp and paper industry is headquartered in a developing country and makes its own machine designs. It is a paper machine manufacturer in Brazil. All others are subsidiaries of or are working under licenses from developed country manufacturers.

Distribution of Production Costs

Whatever technologies are chosen, pulp and paper is very capital intensive when compared to the textile industry. Furthermore even when capital-related costs are put aside, the structure of the remaining costs in the two industries is quite different.

It is commonly accepted in the pulp and paper industry that the minimum economic size for a sulfate pulp mill, with the technologies available at present, is of the order of 400 tons per day of air-dried pulp (pulp with a moisture content of 7 percent). To operate efficiently and at an acceptable pollution level, such a pulp mill would require, besides the main processing equipment, a chemical recovery system, chemical preparation units, including a lime kiln, a power plant, steam generation units, water treatment units, an effluent purification plant, and the necessary infrastructure to transport some 800 tons of wood per day to the mill and ship 400 tons per day of pulp or paper. A bleached sulfate pulp and paper mill of 300-ton-per-day capacity starting production in 1972 (therefore at 1970-1971 equipment prices) had a capital cost of U.S. $500 per annual ton of capacity, excluding interest during construction and working capital. Taking into account a doubling of equipment costs since that time and including the cost of infrastructure, interest during construction, and working capital, such a mill would have required an investment of about U.S. $150 million in 1978, still excluding the cost of forestry operations.

Such a large investment creates only a small number of jobs. Operating continuously on the basis of four shifts, a pulp mill such as the one just described would create only about 270 jobs, most requiring a high degree of skill generally considered scarce in developing countries. The investment cost per job created by such a pulp mill would be about U.S. $750,000.

The scale and capital intensity of the pulp and paper industry become even more obvious when these figures are compared to those of the textile industry. It is considered that the minimum economic size for a short fiber spinning and weaving mill is 15,000 spindles. Such a mill, with the technology generally used in developing countries, would have an investment cost of about U.S. $20 million to $25 million (1978) and would employ some 700 employees on a four-shift basis. The capital cost per job created therefore would be about U.S. $30,000.

Figure 5.3 provides a breakdown of the production cost of a typical pulp mill in six different countries. Table 5.1 provides a comparison of the relative importance of the various inputs to the production costs of the textile and pulp and paper industries. They highlight important findings about production costs in the pulp and paper industry as compared to those of the textile industry.

1. *The predominance of capital-related cost items in pulp and paper production costs.* Capital-related cost items (depreciation, interest/return on capital) accounted for 50 to 60 percent of the total cost of production of the pulp and paper mills visited, versus 40 to 50 percent for textile mills. This proportion tended to be higher among pulp and paper mills in developing countries than among mills of similar capacity and technology in developed countries, even when the same cost of capital was assumed. The cost of a new pulp and paper mill in a developing country tends to be inflated by the larger investment required in infrastructure,

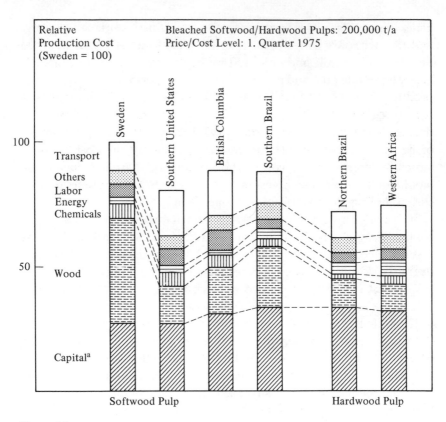

Figure 5.3
Production Cost Comparison of Pulp Mills, by Regions
a. Infrastructure excluded.
Source: Jaakko Poyry & Co., Consulting Engineers.

Table 5.1
Comparison of the Production Cost Structures of Textile and Pulp and Paper
Industries (in percentages)

	Textile[a]	Pulp and Paper[b]
Raw material	30–40	25–30
Consumables	2–5	5–10
Water steam power	2–5	7–10
Labor	10–15	4–6
Depreciation, amortization	20–25	25–30
Interest, return on capital	20–25	25–30
Total production cost	100	100

a. Figures are approximate for a spinning and weaving mill of more than 15,000 spindles operating in a developing country.
b. Figures are approximate for a bleached sulfate pulp and printing and writing paper mill with a capacity of 200 to 300 tons per day operating in a developing country.

the larger transportation costs for imported equipment, and the higher erection cost due to the cost of expatriate specialists brought from developed countries. Lower investments in pollution-abatement facilities were found not to be sufficient to offset these cost-increasing elements.

2. *The importance of chemical and energy costs.* Chemical and energy costs represent 12 to 20 percent of total pulp and paper production costs, while consumables and energy represent only 4 to 10 percent of production costs in the textile industry. These figures in fact largely understate the importance of chemical and energy costs in pulp and paper mills since they account for only the cost of the chemicals and fuel bought by the mill. To obtain the real cost of the chemicals, steam and energy inputs in the pulp and papermaking process, the operating and investment-related costs of the chemical preparation, chemical recovery, and power and steam generating facilities should be added to the cost of the chemicals and fuel bought outside.

3. *The relative unimportance of labor costs.* Labor costs represent only between 4 and 6 percent of total pulp and paper production costs versus 10 to 15 percent in textile. Furthermore in the pulp and paper industry, half of the labor cost is accounted for by the cost of managers, supervisors, engineers, and technicians. Semiskilled and unskilled workers account for only 1 to 2 percent of production cost and less than 5 percent of value added in pulp and paper.

Impact of Economies of Scale on Labor Intensity

The capital-intensive nature of the pulp and paper industry stems from the fact that the transformation of the raw materials is achieved by a chemical process in which the main role of manpower is to control the flows of raw materials and other inputs.

Economies of scale in this industry also stem from the chemical nature of the process.[2] Engineers have used what has become known as the "0.6 rule of thumb" to derive the capital cost of space-enclosing structures and chemical-processing equipment from their processing capacity. This rule is expressed as: $K = a \cdot Q^{0.6}$, where K = capital cost, Q = capacity, and a is a coefficient that depends on the characteristics of the structure. Although this formula has many limitations, it points to a less than proportional increase of cost when the capacity of a tank, processing vessel, or pipe is increased.[3] Because pulp and paper manufacturing facilities comprise a large number of such tanks and processing containers and of pipes connecting them, their investment cost tends to exhibit the same relation to capacity. This makes for the large economies of scale in that industry.

Impact on Labor Use

Since labor performs only a control function, the amount of labor necessary to control one unit of equipment is independent of the size of this unit. In chemical processes an increase in the capacity of a piece of equipment changes neither the number nor the type of the variables to be controlled. Therefore while the nature of the process brings about large economies of scale and pushes toward the adoption of the largest possible unit of production allowed by technical and market limitations, the labor requirement will remain relatively independent of scale. For processing equipment of a given technology the quantity of labor used will be solely a function of the control technology selected. The only manner in which employment would be increased is by having two smaller pieces of equipment instead of one large one perform the same function. But because of economies of scale, the investment cost of two smaller pieces of equipment is greater than that of one large one of the same combined capacity. Since the smaller-unit alternative would use more capital and more labor, it is altogether less efficient and should never be preferred.

Impact on Capital-Labor Trade-Offs

Besides their direct impact on capital-labor ratios, economies of scale have some indirect effects on capital-labor trade-offs. The larger a piece of equipment, the greater is the cost of its downtime since downtime cost is mostly a function of production loss. At the same time the larger a piece of equipment, the larger the quantity of inputs and output to load and unload. As the incentive to minimize downtime increases, so does the importance of performing the loading and unloading operations as rapidly as possible so that another processing cycle can start as quickly as possible. The more labor-intensive methods of loading and unloading a piece of equipment, however, have a capacity per unit of time that is limited by the potential for a worker's physical access to the machine. Once this limit is reached, plant designers must turn to more automated loading and unloading technologies to prevent downtime from increasing proportionally to the capacity of the equipment. It is in fact the same considerations that justify the adoption of continuous rather than batch technologies beyond a certain scale of operation.

Larger scales of operation also make the manual control of some functions extremely difficult, if not impossible. The pressure valves of large reaction vessels operate under such high pressure that they cannot be operated manually. The control valves of pipes that carry a ton of pulp slurry a minute cannot be closed by hand, and chippers that process whole tree trunks cannot be fed manually.

Finally the larger a unit of production, the greater the cost of errors of inefficiencies in the control and programming of this unit's operations. The incentive to adopt methods of control and programming that minimize the risk of such errors will therefore be greater for larger production units. This consideration will undoubtedly play a role in the choice of control technologies no matter what the relative cost of labor and capital may be.

The textile production facilities examined were of a sufficient size for economies of scale not to be a factor in technology choice. In the pulp and paper industry, on the other hand, the effect of economies of scale could not be eliminated. Even if a sample of large-scale pulp and paper manufacturing facilities could be assembled, it would not present an accurate picture of this industry's operating conditions in developing countries. Only three of the twelve pulp and paper production facilities studied operated at or above the minimum economic scale of production of 400 tons per day. In all of these facilities, economies of scale influenced the technology choice decisions directly or indirectly, determining to some extent their relative use of capital and labor.

Impact of Cost of Information on Capital-Labor Trade-Offs

The need to adapt the technology to local conditions as well as the custom-made nature of the equipment make the cost of designing a pulp and paper facility a relatively large portion of total investment costs. Consequently the cost of design itself becomes an item to be minimized. This is usually achieved by limiting the number of alternative technologies considered and by concentrating only on those that deal with crucial variables.

While no more than two to four years normally will elapse between an initial decision to fund a textile project and the start-up of the facilities, the same process will take a minimum of five and sometimes as long as ten years in the pulp and paper industry. Soil surveys, forest inventories, growing tests, pulping tests, and equipment designing are complex and enormously time-consuming tasks. The costs incurred during that phase of a project represent a large share of its total investment cost. Figure 5.4 contains a breakdown of the investment costs of a typical pulp and paper mill. The costs classified under "others" are mostly study, design, and engineering costs—in other words the necessary engineering, preproject expenses, project administration, start-up, and financial charges before start-up cost items. These represent 25 percent of total fixed investment in Sweden and 30 percent in Brazil. As table 5.2 shows, those same project evaluation, engineering, and preoperating cost categories accounted for only 10 to 15 percent of the total project cost of a textile mill.

Because of the relative contribution of design and engineering to overall project cost, pulp and paper firms attach a great deal of importance to the control and possible trimming of these cost items. To achieve this, firms will attempt to shorten the evaluation and engineering phase, eliminate tests that are not considered crucial, and reduce to a minimum the number of alternative project designs being studied. Capital-labor trade-offs are not an aspect of project design that ranks high in their order of priorities. Consequently alternative project configurations that are only justified in terms of potential for such trade-offs tend to be eliminated.

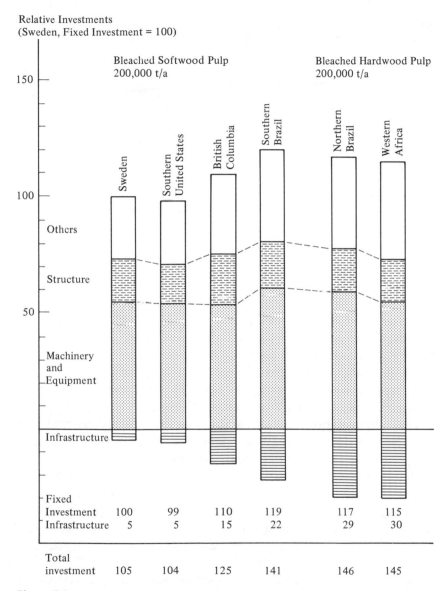

Figure 5.4
Relative Investment Requirements of Pulp Mills in Some Production Areas
Source: Jaakko Poyry & Co., Consulting Engineers.

Table 5.2
Comparison of the Project Cost Structure of Textile and Pulp and Paper Industries (in percentages)

	Textile[a]	Pulp and Paper[b]
Infrastructure and site development	2–3	2–3
Civil engineering and buildings	15–20	15–20
Machinery and equipment	60–65	40–45
Erection	3–4	10–15
Engineering, preoperating expenses, start-up	4–8	15–20
Interest during construction	5–10	10–15

Note: Land cost and working capital have been excluded. Project cost does not include forestry operations.
a. Figures are approximate for a spinning and weaving mill of more than 15,000 spindles installed in a developing country.
b. Figures are approximate for a bleached sulfate pulp and printing and writing paper mill of a capacity of 200 to 300 tons per day installed in a developing country.

Furthermore to reduce design costs, pulp and paper firms try to adapt existing designs and technologies to their needs rather than to develop completely new ones. This further reduces the propensity of these firms to adapt to capital and labor costs in developing countries since designs adapted to such cost structures have not yet been given much attention. These countries have not constituted a significant market for pulp and paper equipment manufacturers and design firms. Consequently these firms have had little incentive to adapt their technologies and designs to the specific conditions of developing countries.

Neither have these countries developed an indigenous design and equipment manufacturing capability on their own. While artisans have been engaged in spinning and weaving in most developing countries for as long as they have in Europe, wood-based papermaking is a completely new activity, without established traditions in developing countries.

Eventually some of these handicaps might be overcome. In contrast to developed countries, which are faced with pollution problems and limited wood resources, some developing countries offer large wood resources and tree growing rates up to three times as fast. A possible shift might already have begun. Between 1963 and 1974, 8 percent of the world increase in wood pulp capacity and 15 percent of the paper capacity increase took place in developing countries, a third of it in Latin America.

The Critical Nature of Inputs and Capital-Labor Trade-Offs

The choice of technology in the pulp and paper industry involves complex and sensitive trade-offs between numerous inputs. In contrast the choice between alternative technologies in the textile industry was shown to involve trade-offs between the use of capital and of labor that have little effect on raw material usage and a predictable impact on power usage. In the pulp and paper industry alternative technologies entail different consumptions of chemicals, steam, and power and result in different wood yields. This is in addition to the trade-offs these alternatives may imply between capital and labor. Ideally this added complexity should not change the criterion for technology choice. The technology chosen should still be the one that results in the lowest production cost even though labor cost might no longer be crucial to the choice.

Basing a technology choice on the criterion of production cost minimization, however, is impractical in the pulp and paper industry for two reasons. First, the custom-made nature of equipment and production processes makes it virtually impossible to estimate all of the possible trade-offs between the different inputs. This leads to even greater difficulties in tracking down their interrelationships. Second, the cost in management and engineering time associated with the acquisition of this information is too large to allow much investigation of alternatives. Thus the tendency of most pulp and paper manufacturers is to concentrate on the efficiency of use of a few crucial inputs and only seek trade-offs between these rather than on attempting a global optimization.

The share of total production cost that an input represents and its significance in the determination of the efficiency of the whole process are used as the basic criteria for determining its overall importance to the project. Discussions with the management of the pulp and paper firms studied and with the staff of the design and consulting firms pointed to a clear ranking of the relative importance of these various inputs. In order of importance, the resulting considerations are: machine efficiency; wood yield; chemicals, steam, and power usage; and labor usage.

Machine Efficiency

Machine efficiency is the most crucial element in the determination of a mill's overall efficiency because it can be subject to wide variations and because of the importance of capital-related costs in the total cost of production. It is the most important variable in production cost minimization and therefore receives the most attention in the design of a pulp and paper mill.

Pulp and paper mills normally operate year round on a four-shift basis. Production is halted only for maintenance purposes, in case of breakdown, or when there is a change in the raw material to be used or the type of product to be made. Because of the importance of fixed costs, a 10 percent reduction in machine efficiency should normally result in an increase in production cost of at least 5 percent. Furthermore the complexity and sensitivity of pulp and paper manufacturing processes can cause frequent breakdowns. Thus mills can sharply differ from each other in the machine efficiency they reach. While North American and northern European mills often operate at 110 percent of nominal capacity, it is not unusual for mills to operate far below capacity in developing countries because of design problems or bad maintenance. In the choice of a technology, foremost attention is therefore given to equipment reliability and to ensuring that the equipment chosen can operate a maximum efficiency.

Wood Yield

Pulp and papermaking consists of removing a certain amount of lignin from the wood and arranging the remaining cellulose fibers into a sheet. The yield of the process is the percentage of the weight of the processed wood that is represented by the paper or paperboard produced. Yield therefore should be a function of the percentage of cellulosic material contained in the wood used as a raw material and of the percentage of the noncellulosic part of the raw material that is removed by the pulping process. The latter is itself a function of the pulping agent used and of the pulping conditions. In practice, however, the yield is also affected by the amount of pulp slurry—and particularly of the valuable cellulosic component of this slurry—that is lost in the pulping and papermaking process. Such losses can occur because of damage done to the cellulose fibers by too harsh a mechanical treatment in the refining or defibrizing steps, because of imperfectly adjusted screens, because of leaks or overflows in the production process, or because of imperfect recycling of the rejects at the different stages of processing.

The sensitive nature and complexity of the process lead to wide variations in the value of these parameters and therefore in the overall yield of the process. In the pulp and paper industry these variations in yield play a much larger role in the determination of unit production costs than in the textile industry. Yield differences have an important impact on production costs because of the large share of these costs accounted for by the raw material. To this raw material cost should also be added the value of the machine production capacity and of chemicals that were used before the raw material loss occurred. Consequently fiber yield is a critical factor in process efficiency. Its value, and the trade-offs its maximization implies, were found to be important considerations in the choice-of-technology decision.

Chemicals, Steam, and Power Usage

These are the next most important considerations in the choice of technology. The reason is not so much the variable costs embodied in the consumption of these inputs as it is the investment cost associated with the building of chemical preparation, chemical recuperation, and steam and power generating capacities.

A less than efficient use of chemicals, steam, and power increases the quantity of these inputs required to keep the plant operating at full capacity. Since pulp and paper plants produce most of the chemicals and all of the power and steam they use, larger production facilities of these inputs need to be constructed. Such inefficiencies therefore lead to increases in the already large capital investment required.

Since power and steam cannot be economically stored before their use, surges in the need of these inputs would also require the installation of larger production capacities. When designing alternative technologies, not only will much attention be given to the reduction of chemicals, power, and steam consumption but also to the elimination of surges in power and steam requirements.

Labor Usage

Machine efficiency, fiber yield, and chemical and energy consumption will play a major role in the design of and choice between alternative technologies or project configurations due to the importance of the factors of production whose usage they measure as well as their significance in the determination of a mill's overall efficiency. Most of the analysis of alternative choices therefore is devoted to evaluating these three variables. Possible trade-offs between the factors of production whose usage they measure will also be investigated.

Labor usage, on the other hand, is neither an important manufacturing cost nor a crucial one in determining the mill's overall efficiency. It will therefore tend to be viewed as a result of the technology choice rather than as a direct factor in this choice. The technologies chosen to optimize the value of the three crucial elements might use more or less labor than the alternatives considered, but they will not tend to be chosen because of this larger or smaller labor usage.

6

The Pulp and Paper Industry: How Technology Choices Were Made

Even though cost minimization is a more complex criterion in the pulp and paper than in the textile industry, it is still only one of the considerations that influence technology choice. As was the case in the textile industry, other considerations entered into the decision-making process, steering the choice away from cost-minimizing technologies. In contrast with the textile industry, these considerations were different depending on whether a technology was being chosen for main processing equipment, for handling equipment, or for control devices. Such a differentiation is already apparent in the process followed to make technology choice decisions.

The Decision Process

In the pulp and paper industry it is impossible to separate the choice-of-technology decision process from the procedures leading to the decision to invest and to the choice of the scale and profile of the production facility. In the textile industry, in contrast, the technology decision could be isolated from the other choices made by managers while evaluating and planning a new facility.

In textile the choice of output characteristics and volume, the decision to invest, and the choice of production technologies are roughly sequential. First a potential market is identified, leading to the definition of an investment opportunity. An evaluation of this investment opportunity follows on the basis of rough estimations of its costs and benefits. It is at this stage that a decision whether to seize that opportunity will be made. If the decision is to go ahead with the project, the process of choosing production technologies will start and proceed along the lines already described. A pure sequential representation of the investment process of the textile industry is, of course, an oversimplification; there might in fact be some backtracking among the three processes.

In the pulp and paper industry, on the other hand, the investment decision process in no way can be described in sequential terms. It is not even possible to determine whether a potential project exists before a technology capable of transforming the wood available into the paper that is sought has been developed. It is also not possible to judge the profitability of such a project before the consumption of steam, power, and chemicals has been determined with precision. Colombia provides a typical example of a situation in which no project potential existed before the development of a new technology. There previously was no known way to utilize the wood available from the tropical forests there to satisfy the local demand for cardboard boxes. The company that now transforms the wood from these forests into cardboard first had to develop a technique for the pulping of mixed tropical hardwoods. Clearly the choice of technology decision process in the pulp and paper industry encompasses the whole investment analysis process—from the early identification stage to the final negotiation of contracts with equipment manufacturers.

A general description of the investment analysis process for the pulp and paper industry is provided in figure 6.1. Figure 6.2 contains a description of the choice-of-technology aspect of this process, together with an attempt to define the role of the different organizations that participate in it.

Identification

The identification of a situation that constitutes a project opportunity may come in several ways. The company might have developed a technique, such as the pulping of mixed tropical hardwood, that it wants to apply in different places in order to spread its research costs. It may want to enter a large and developing market such as Brazil. Or perhaps it wishes to secure access to promising potential sources of raw materials such as the island of Kalimantan (formerly Borneo). From this identification stage a general definition of the project will emerge; it will include the proposed source of wood, the types of products contemplated, and the anticipated scale of production.

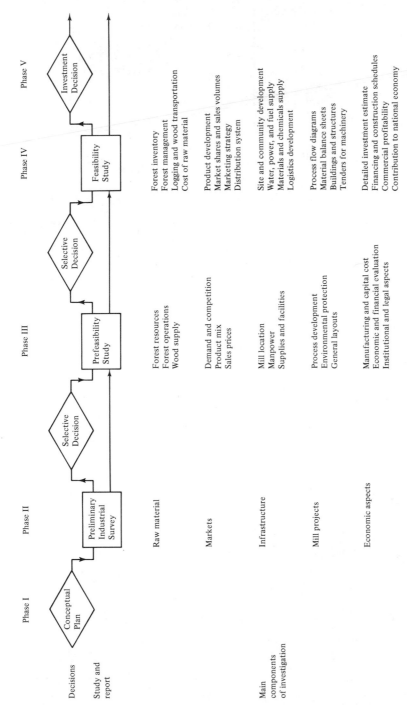

Figure 6.1
Investment Analysis Process in the Pulp and Paper Industry
Source: Jaakko Poyry & Co., Consulting Engineers.

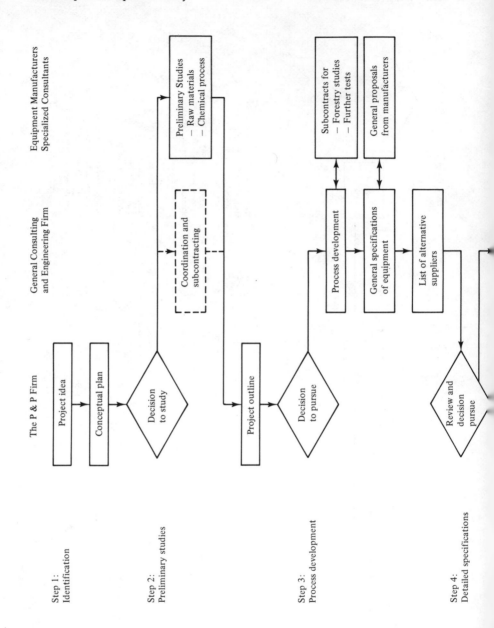

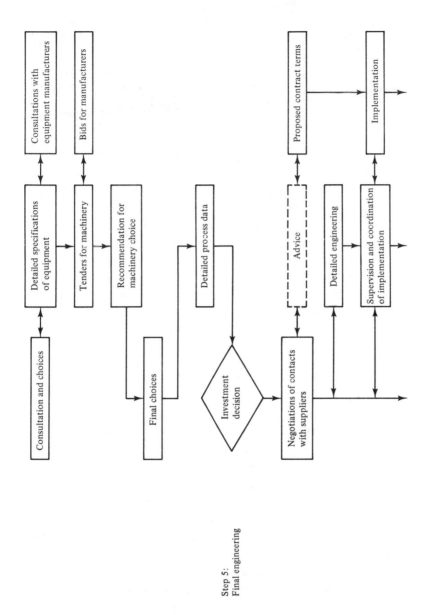

Step 5:
Final engineering

Figure 6.2
Choice-of-Technology Decision Process in the Pulp and Paper Industry

Preliminary Studies

The next step is to define the technical parameters of this project opportunity. These deal mostly with two subjects: the wood supply and the chemical transformation process. If the project is to use natural forests as its source of raw material, inquiries must deal with the species of wood available, its chemical properties, and the area that will have to be harvested to provide a continuous supply of wood for a mill of the scale contemplated. If the project is to grow its own wood supply, soil analysis, growth rate studies of different species, and planting and logging schedules have to be made.

The characteristics of the wood to be used and the volume in which it is expected to be available will allow for an identification of the process (or processes) to be employed in order to obtain a paper of given characteristics at the lowest cost. To assess the response of the type of wood available to different pulping processes, pulping tests will often be made, either in other plants of the company or in laboratories. Through these tests a first evaluation of the chemical requirements of the mill will be made. At this stage, however, the pulping process will be defined only in general terms (such as sulfate or sulfite), and neither the exact sequence of processing steps nor the types of equipment to be used will have been determined yet.

These preliminary studies are generally conducted with the assistance of outside consultants. Although the largest pulp and paper firms might have the capacity to do these studies internally, they prefer to use outside consultants to avoid overburdening their internal research and design capacity. By using outside consultants, a firm also secures an independent opinion and takes advantage of the pool of knowledge accumulated by organizations that are dealing with all of the main pulp and paper equipment manufacturers and that therefore could have a better knowledge of recent industry developments.

On the basis of the broad project description developed at this stage, it will be decided whether to pursue a more detailed analysis of the project. A selection might also be made among different investment opportunities or alternative project concepts. Even at such an early stage, however, the number of alternative project concepts considered is generally quite limited since the raw materials available and the market opportunities determine to a large extent the main characteristics of the potential project.

Process Development

The third stage in the evaluation process may be called the prefeasibility stage. As far as technology choice is concerned, it is at this stage that the development of the production process takes place. The help of a general pulp and paper consulting and engineering firm becomes indispensable from this stage on. This consulting firm might subcontract some specialized aspects of the inquiry, such as forestry studies or the testing of pulping and bleaching reactions, to specialized firms or research institutes.

The task of the general consultant is to refine the project description developed previously and arrive at a precise process outline. This outline shows the main characteristics of the transformations performed and defines in general terms the equipment required in each of the processing steps. The consulting firm generally prepares this outline by drawing on its accumulated knowledge about equipment that can be manufactured by different suppliers. Sometimes preliminary contacts with equipment manufacturers are initiated in order for these manufacturers to propose technical solutions to specific problems.

At this stage the technology choices for the processing equipment are made. Since detailed specifications have not yet been developed, these choices are based on rough estimates of input requirements. Thus only the most crucial variables in the efficiency of the process are investigated and influence the selection.

A list of equipment suppliers that can supply the types of equipment required by the mill might also be drawn up. For most pieces of equipment, however, this is not necessary since the technical choices made about the process and the overall equipment specifications developed reduce this list to a very short one, if not a single name.

At this point the elements needed for a preliminary evaluation of the investment cost, the manufacturing cost, and the profitability of the proposed venture are available. On the basis of these estimates the project sponsors will decide whether to proceed to the final stage of analysis, to abandon the project, or to redirect it by changing some of the basic assumptions on which it has been conceived. Redirecting the project, however, means that some of the analysis already performed will have to be redone.

Detailed Specifications

In the feasibility study stage of the project evaluation, a detailed definition of the different aspects of the project is made, from logging schedules to financial projections. From the production technology side this entails developing detailed specifications for all of the equipment required on the basis of process flow and material balance computations. This is normally done by the general consulting firm in conjunction with both the project sponsors and the equipment suppliers. Once the detailed equipment specifications have been worked out, bids are requested from the manufacturers.

The terms of these bids are generally defined by the consultant, who will also review the submissions. For technical as well as economic reasons competitive bidding by several manufacturers is the exception rather than the rule in the pulp and paper industry. The submission of a bid for large pieces of equipment such as digesters, recovery boilers, evaporation towers, and paper machines involves so much engineering work that a manufacturer cannot reasonably be expected to incur these costs without some assurance of an order.

After the bids are received and analyzed, detailed process data will be generated. It is then possible to make precise estimates of investment and production costs and, on the basis of these, develop a set of revised and far more reliable financial projections that are critical to the sponsors' final investment decision.

Therefore it is only very late in the planning and design of a pulp and paper mill that precise cost and input requirement estimates can be made. To generate the detailed specifications needed for such estimates, extremely large amounts of time and money must be spent. At this stage only drastic discoveries would result in changes in the project's design. Choices such as those dealing with technology have to be made much earlier and are therefore based on approximate data.

Detailed Engineering and Implementation

The decision to proceed with the project does not mark the end of the engineering studies nor of the technical-definition process. The final negotiations with the equipment suppliers that are initiated at this point include a definition of the last technical details of the equipment. It is also at this stage that the instrumentation and control equipment for the mill is defined precisely. On the basis of these exact descriptions and specifications, the detailed engineering of the plant is made by the general consultant. This same consultant will then coordinate and supervise construction, training of the workers, testing, and start-up and commissioning.

The Choice of Technology for Processing Equipment

Processing equipment is defined as all of the machinery that transforms the product or one of its inputs. It excludes handling and transfer equipment, as well as instrumentation and control systems.

Scale of Production Considerations

The choice-of-technology decision for processing equipment was found to be primarily a function of scale considerations. The relative efficiency of the alternative machine technologies identified earlier proved to be a function of scale rather than of the cost of the factors of production.
    The factor requirements of these alternative processing technologies can be determined only by means of extensive testing and lengthy design effort, making it impossible to arrive at a systematic, quantitative appraisal of the impact of scale on their relative efficiency. For the most important processing steps it is, however, possible to estimate this relationship between scale and relative efficiency of alternative technologies, as well as its impact on capital labor usage.

Digesting Step

There are two basic alternative technologies in the digesting step: batch digesting and continuous digesting. Batch digesters are characterized by a low capital cost because they are nothing more than large pressure vessels in which wood chips and chemicals are mixed and then subjected to high temperature and pressure before being drained off for further processing. Continuous digesters, on the other hand, have a much higher capital cost for the same processing capacity. They incorporate sophisticated feeding mechanisms capable of introducing wood chips and chemicals into a vessel that is constantly kept at high pressure and temperature. Continuous digesters also require an internal transport mechanism capable of carrying the wood chips through the digester while they are submitted to the various phases of the cooking cycle. Unloading of the output is also done in a continuous manner by means of a mechanism that prevents a loss of pressure or heat from the digester.

At a given scale of production the main advantage of the continuous technology is that it operates without surges in demand for wood, chemicals, steam pressure, and heat and in supply of digested pulp. The elimination of surges, in turn, allows for a reduction in the planned capacity of the facilities that produce these inputs or in the need for intermediate storage capacity. The investment required in such facilities is therefore reduced.

How does scale of production influence the relative efficiency of these two technologies? The answer is that while the cost of a digester, whether batch or continuous, increases less than proportionally to its processing capacity, batch digesters have a maximum capacity of 80 to 120 tons per day while continuous digesters can have a daily capacity of up to 1,200 tons. Therefore the investment cost of a daily ton of continuous digesting capacity decreases until 1,200 tons of daily capacity, while that of batch digesting capacity remains roughly constant above 120-ton-per-day capacity. It is estimated that for a plant with a 250-ton-per-day capacity, the capital cost of installing three batch digesters or one continuous digester is roughly equal. For a plant with a 500-ton-per-day capacity, however, the capital cost of one continuous digester is 25 to 30 percent lower than the cost of five batch digesters. This gap between the capital cost of the batch and the continuous alternatives keeps widening as the scale of operation increases up to 1,200 tons per day, the maximum capacity of a continuous digester.

Trade-offs between capital and labor in the pulp and paper industry are to be found in the choice of instrumentation and control equipment rather than in the choice of technology for the processing equipment. This is clearly the case in the digesting step. Whether batch or continuous digesting is selected, a choice must be made regarding the degree of automation of the instruments and controls that will equip these digesters. The range of available alternatives extends from the separate manual control of each digester's individual functions to the integration of the digesting step into a computer control system for the entire pulp mill.

This does not mean, however, that the choice between batch and continuous digesters—while itself mainly dependent upon the scale of operations—does not have important implications as to the amount of employment created by each of the alternative control technologies. All available control technologies may be used to operate batch as well as continuous digesters, but the amount of employment each would generate depends upon the type of digester whose operations it governs.

Table 6.1
Number of Operators per Shift Required for Digesting Step of Mills of Various Capacities and Technologies

Capacity	250 Tons per Day		500 Tons per Day	
Control technology	Alternative 2 Manual on Location	Alternative 5 Automatic Step Panel	Alternative 2 Manual on Location	Alternative 5 Automatic Step Panel
Batch digesters	3	1	5	1
Continuous digester	2	1	2	1

Note: See table 2.3 for a more detailed definition of alternative technology levels.

In other words the choice between batch and continuous digesters sets a range for the number of jobs that can be created by the instrumentation and control decision. Table 6.1 indicates the number of operators required by a 250-ton-per-day and a 500-ton-per-day digesting step equipped with either batch or continuous digesters, for two alternative levels of sophistication of control equipment.

The manual control of one batch digester, regardless of size, requires one operator; the manual control of one continuous digester, also regardless of size, requires one operator and one helper. Therefore under the manual option, larger plants require more batch digesters, and as a consequence more workers. But, if equipped with a continuous digester, a larger digester can be used without any change in employment. The automatic control of the digesting step from a step control panel requires one operator, regardless of the digester technology adopted and of the number of digesters. With this control technology the amount of employment generated in the digesting step is therefore independent of the capacity of the mill. Consequently, as table 6.1 shows, batch digesters tend to offer a wider range of capital-labor trade-offs in the choice of instrumentation and control technologies than do continuous digesters. Efforts to take advantage of economies of scale through the choice of processing equipment result in this case in a narrowing of the scope of possible adaptation to differences in the relative cost of capital and labor.

Papermaking Step
Another example of the way in which economies of scale influence the relative efficiency of alternative technologies, and thereby fix the

range of economically feasible capital-labor mixes, can be found in the papermaking step. A number of technological innovations in papermaking machinery have made possible increases in machine speed and machine width, thereby allowing for much higher production capacities per machine. The labor requirement, on the other hand, is about the same—at a given level of instrumentation and control technology—for all paper machines whatever their production capacity may be. Depending upon the instrumentation and control technology adopted, between five and ten workers are needed to operate a paper machine. The relationship between price and production capacity of paper machines, however, is such that to obtain a given volume of production, it is more economical to install one paper machine of a newer technology than two of an older, simpler technology and half the capacity each. From the employment-creation point of view, the one paper machine solution will require half the number of operators and two-thirds the total employment of the two machine solution. (The percentage reduction in total employment that the one paper machine alternative represents over the two paper machine alternative is smaller than the percentage reduction in the number of operators because these two options require the same number of highly skilled maintenance workers.)

Table 6.2 presents a comparison of the investment and labor cost increases associated with increases in machine width and speed. It also provides a comparison of investment and labor costs of the two alternatives for a given production level: one fast and wide machine (column D) versus two slow and narrow machines (column E).

Overall Impact
The economic advantage that larger processing units hold in the papermaking step was found to be quite common in the pulp and paper industry and to exist in most other processing steps. It is less expensive, if technically feasible, to buy one large piece of equipment capable of processing all of the mill's needs than two pieces of equipment of half that capacity for the recovery boiler, the evaporation towers, the lime kiln, and several other main pieces of processing equipment. This investment-cost comparison is all the more true when building costs are included in the cost estimates. At the same time the number of operators needed for a given instrumentation and control technology is proportional to the number of units (except in the case of automatic centrally located controls that operate all of the pieces of equipment of a processing step or mill section—technology levels 5, 6, and 7 in

Table 6.2
Increases in Machine Cost and Employment Associated with Increases in Paper
Machine Size

	A	B	C	D	2 machines E[a]
Speed (feet per mn)	1,250	1,250	1,700	1,700	1,000
Width trim (inches)	244	305	244	305	244
Production theoretical (t/day)	195	243	265	330	312
Efficiency (%)	94.5	94.5	90	90	95.5
Production actual (t/day)	184	230	239	298	298
Production actual (index)	100	125	130	162	162
Machine Cost (index)	100	111	113	124	185
Operating labor cost (index)	100	102.5	107	110	195
Maintenance labor cost (index)	100	121.5	132	164	170
Total labor cost (index)	100	106	112	120	190

Note: Estimates made on the basis of an identical instrumentation and control technology
being used in all the cases.
a. Two machines.

table 2.3) rather than to the unit's size. The impact of such economies
of scale on the amount of employment that results from the application
of the same control technology in mills of different size is shown for
an entire pulp mill in table 6.3.

Flexibility and Risk Considerations

While cost considerations justify the choice of the largest possible processing units, given technical and market constraints, two noncost considerations temper such a tendency.

The first consideration that argues for the adoption of several small
units rather than one large one is flexibility of production. Paper consumption in developing countries is low. In 1975 developing countries,
with a population more than twice that of developed countries, con-
sumed only 11.8 million of the total 133 million tons of paper and
paperboard produced in the world. For this reason pulp and paper
mills in developing countries must produce a much wider range of
paper types than developed countries' mills in order to attain minimum
economies of scale. If they were to use large units with high production
capacities, these mills would have to stop production often in order to

Table 6.3
Scale of Production and Employment Generation in Bleached Sulfate Pulp Mills

Production capacity (t/day)	150	225	300	450	600
Production capacity index	100	150	200	300	400
Total investment index	100	122	148	187	234
Total employment index	100	127	140	165	180

Note: Estimates made on the basis of identical instrumentation and control technology being used in all cases.

clean and readjust these units before starting production of a different product type. Although small and more numerous units are more expensive to buy and operate, they have the advantage of providing savings on downtime by allowing specialization of the different units in the production of the various types of pulp or paper required.

This consideration was found to play an important role in the selection of technology for digesters and paper machines. Managers of medium-sized pulp and paper plants in developing countries producing for the local market stressed the importance of this consideration in explaining their choice of several batch digesters rather than of one continuous digester and of several small paper machines rather than one large one. In contrast export-oriented mills opted for one large digester and one large paper machine because they were able to specialize in the production of one type of pulp and paper.

The second consideration that tends to justify the choice of several small units rather than one large one is risk minimization. If one piece of equipment must fulfill the needs of an entire mill and this unit breaks down, the mill is inoperative until that unit can be started up again. If several pieces of equipment operating in parallel perform that same operation, it is highly unlikely that all of them will break down at the same time. In fact by somewhat overburdening the other units and rescheduling maintenance stoppages, it is often possible to make up for the temporary loss of production capacity in one step and to keep the rest of the mill operating at full capacity. For the same reason batch processing technologies equipped with intermediate storage facilities between processing steps are often preferred to continuous processing technologies. In case of a short breakdown in one step, the rest of the production process can continue operating at full capacity by processing some of the intermediate product in storage.

Because of a lower overall level of training of the workers and of a scarcity of good maintenance personnel, planners and managers of pulp and paper facilities in developing countries felt much less confident of being able to avoid breakdowns than their developed countries' counterparts. Lack of support services and distance from the equipment suppliers also increased the time required in developing countries to repair such breakdowns. For these reasons risk minimization considerations were found to have played an important role in the choice of smaller units and discontinuous processes by the firms studied. The importance of risk minimization considerations was confirmed by the fact that in some crucial processing steps where a processing unit can be added at a reasonable cost, several plants installed one more unit than was actually needed. Such was the case in the digesting step when batch digesters were used.

The effects of flexibility improvement and risk minimization are difficult to dissociate from each other. They have the same influence on the choice-of-technology decision and are usually found together, except in the case of mills producing for export. Taken together they seem to have most influenced the choice of processing technology among medium-sized mills. While large-sized mills (above 400-ton-per-day capacity) were found to have always chosen the large, continuous units option, medium-sized mills (250 to 400 tons per day) were found in all cases but one to have selected the small, more numerous units. Pure cost of production considerations still favored the large, continuous unit alternative in these medium-sized installations. It appears, however, that in their case the production costs of the two alternatives were considered close enough for flexibility and risk considerations to tip the scales in favor of the small-units option. For large-sized mills, on the other hand, the cost advantage of large, continuous units appears to have been too important for flexibility and risk considerations to affect the decision.

The Choice of Technology for Materials Handling Equipment

Handling and transfer operations can be divided into four groups: the handling of the wood in the wood yard, the transfer of the chips between the chippers and the digesters, the transfer of the pulp among the various pulp processing steps, and the handling of the paper at the end of the paper machine. Theoretically all of these can be performed manually, and this is the way the handling was in fact done a century ago. Pulp from the digesters, for example, was dumped on the floor of the pulp mill after cooking, and workers would then roll it to the next step in wheelbarrows.

Increases in the scale of production, as well as stricter health and safety standards, have made the manual transfer of the pulp impractical, even for very small mills. The manual loading of chips into the digesters has also become uneconomical because of the relatively low cost of automatic loading systems and because of the increase in the cost and length of downtime that would result from the use of manual loading methods on digesters of larger and larger capacity. The increase in the size of the paper rolls that came about with increases in the speed of the paper machines have made their manual handling physically impossible. Furthermore automatic paper-handling techniques make it possible to unload the paper machine without stopping it and therefore without loss of productivity. There again increases in the speed and width of the paper machines have resulted in an increase in the cost associated with any stoppage of the machine, thus making nonautomatic handling equipment uneconomical.

In the wood yard, on the other hand, a considerable amount of adaptation to the relatively low cost of labor in developing countries is still possible. Nevertheless it was found that the larger the mill, the less labor intensive the technologies adopted to perform wood yard operations tend to become. In mills of less than 100-tons-per-day capacity, all wood yard operations, including in some cases the debarking of the trees, were performed manually or with simple equipment such as handcarts. In contrast mills of 400-tons-per-day capacity or more, confronted with the same factor prices, used cranes and moving belts for these operations. The explanation given by the managers of these large mills is the existence of diseconomies of scale in the use of the labor-intensive methods above a certain volume of operations. The manual unloading of the larger trucks required to supply large mills takes longer and reduces the efficiency of use of these trucks. Since the height to which wood can be stacked manually is limited, the wood yard must also be expanded, resulting in a longer average journey to the chipper. The practical capacity of a chipper is usually determined by the speed at which it can be fed. The physical movement of workers around the unit imposes a fairly low limit of the speed of manual feeding. Once this limit is reached, the choice is to install a second chipper or to shift to automatic feeding.

In cases where it was possible to compute the processing cost of the alternative handling technologies, management choices seemed to be justified on pure economic grounds. No significant biases toward greater capital intensity or labor intensity than economically justified were found in these choices. Three characteristics of wood yard operations explain this readiness to adapt to local factor prices. First, the wood yard normally operates on two shifts and is separated from the rest of the process by a large inventory of wood chips. Therefore any shortfall in the wood yard output does not immediately affect the rest of the process and can easily be made up by overtime work. Second, the operations performed in the wood yard are such that workers' mistakes are of little consequence. Finally when performed manually, the wood yard operations may be subcontracted to outside firms that handle worker relations. Such subcontracting isolates the firm from some of the risks and problems associated with a large labor force.

The Choice of Technology for Instrumentation and Control

The choice of instrumentation and control systems is the main source of capital-labor trade-offs in the pulp and paper industry. One would therefore expect the choice of instrumentation and control technology to be made on the basis of comparisons between the cost of labor and the cost of the equipment that can replace this labor. Instead management's concern with the risk of worker error and the supply of instrument maintenance workers turned out to be the overriding considerations in deciding on the degree of complexity and automation of this equipment. While concern about the risk of worker error tended to promote the choice of more centralized and automated controls, this thrust toward automation was limited by the scarcity of maintenance personnel. The balance struck between these two conflicting considerations seemed to hinge upon the characteristics of the processing step for which the choice was being made, as well as upon the scale of production.

Cost of Human Error

The large-scale nature of the pulp and paper industry and the sensitivity of the process equilibrium make a control error potentially very costly. The consensus in the industry is that such an error or faulty timing is more likely if the control function is performed by a worker than if it is performed automatically, provided that the instruments and automation mechanisms are properly maintained. Moreover it is generally agreed that where manual controls are involved, the risk of error increases with the number of workers involved in this control function. Thus the risk of error is considered greater when several workers manually operate controls located on the equipment itself (alternative technology 1) than if these instruments and controls are centralized at one control panel and operated by a single worker (alternative 3). Yet even this technology is perceived as being more prone to error than one in which these controls are automatically activated when the measured variables reach preset values (technology 4), assuming proper maintenance of these automatic mechanisms.

Theoretically the risk of error should be incorporated in the economic evaluation of different instrumentation and control technologies. By estimating the probability of an error's occurrence during a given time period, as well as the cost of such an error, an expected cost of workers' errors would be obtained. This cost should then be added to the cost of the labor-intensive technology before it is compared to the more capital-intensive one. Such a procedure was followed when the cost of a possible error was thought to be relatively small. In that event a more or less formalized computation of the expected cost of an error would enter the evaluation of alternative technologies. When the cost of an error was considered to be large, the likelihood of its occurrence no longer seemed to play a role in the decision; the manual control alternative would be discarded.

Although managers could not identify what they considered large costs of error, an examination of their choice of control technology decisions revealed some clear criteria. In the plants visited an error whose cost would be considered large and therefore unacceptable was one that could result in serious injury to the workers. For example, vessels operating under high pressure and temperatures normally would have their pressure automatically controlled; the level of corrosive chemicals in tanks would also be automatically controlled; and dangerous operations, such as couching when the paper machine is started, would be automated. A second type of error whose cost was considered excessive was one that would have consequences not only for the processing step in which it occurred but for other steps as well. Such errors would be those that take place in pieces of equipment that play a crucial role in the manufacturing process. As in the textile industry a piece of equipment is considered crucial if it is important in determining the quality of the end product or if it processes the entire production of the plant. Continuous digesters are an example of such pieces of equipment. They are crucial in the determination of the quality of the pulp and normally process the entire plant's output. Batch digesters, on the other hand, are generally considered less crucial since several of them usually operate in parallel. This explains the higher level of automation found among continuous digesters than among batch digesters.

Availability of Instrument Technicians

The maintenance of automatic instruments and controls is felt to require a high degree of skill and a long period of training, even in developed countries. Such skills are rare in developing countries, no matter what price a firm is willing to pay, short of bearing the cost of expatriates. This difficulty in finding qualified personnel for the maintenance of instruments and automatic control systems affects the choice of instrumentation and control technology in an opposite manner than human error. It motivates the adoption of simple, labor-intensive systems in much the same way as the risk of human error promotes the adoption of automated systems. Instrument and control equipment malfunctions resulting from inadequate maintenance are associated with costs in the same way as human errors are.

To limit the extent of such maintenance problems, the firms that were investigated avoided adopting the most sophisticated instrumentation and control systems. Computer-controlled systems, for example, were never considered to be a viable alternative because of the extremely high level of skill required from the maintenance and operating personnel. Firms were also found to rank processing steps in terms of the priority given to their automation and to automate them in that order according to what they felt was the availability of qualified maintenance personnel. This order of priority was consistent with the definition of crucial steps. Therefore firms with access to a larger supply of personnel with maintenance skills would tend to automate a larger number of operations than would firms faced with difficulties in obtaining these skills. For example, some firms would increase the level of automation of their plants on the occasion of an expansion. Such choices are explained by the fact that at the time of the expansion, these firms had already developed their maintenance work force and therefore felt more confident in adopting a higher level of automation.

Table 6.4
Control Technologies Used by Different Types of Pulp and Paper Mills

Processing Step	Control Variable	Alternative** 1	Alternative 2	Alternative 3	Alternative 4	Alternative 5	Alternative 6	Alternative 7
Digester	Chip feeding	@ 0	#					×
	Flow of liquor		@ 0	#				×
	Flow of steam		0		@	#		×
	Unloading of digester	@	0	#				×
	Cycle control			@ 0		#		
Blow tank	Pressure control			@ 0		#		×
	Flow of water			@	0	#		×
	Outflow of pulp			@ 0		#		×
Defiberizers	Flow of pulp	@ 0			#		×	
	Speed of surfaces	@ 0			#		×	
	Pressure	@ 0			#		×	
Screens	Flow of pulp	@ 0			#		×	
	Pressure	@ 0			#		×	
Washers	Flow of pulp	@ 0		#			×	
	Flow of water	@ 0			#		×	
	Speed of drums	@ 0		#			×	

Paper machine	×	#	@	0
Inlet control	×	#	@	0
Vacuum in suction boxes	×	#	@	0
Pressure of felts	×	#	@	0
Steam in dryers	×	#	@	0
Calender rolls pressure	×	#	@	0

× Large (600 t/day) U.S. mill
Large (400 t/day) privately owned mill in developing country.
@ Small (50 t/day) privately owned mill in developing country.
0 Small (35 t/day) government-owned mill in developing country.

Notes: Mills described in this table are mills studied in our field research which were considered as typical of the mills in their category. Only a few processing steps and control variables are described in this table.
For description of alternatives, see table 2.3.

Examples of Control Technology Choices

Table 6.4 compares the typical choices of instrumentation and control technology of a large (600 tons per day) pulp and paper mill located in the United States with those made in developing countries by a large (400 tons per day), a privately owned small (50 tons per day), and a small (35 tons per day) government-owned pulp and paper mill. Several conclusions can be drawn from these technology profiles.

The comparison of the profile of the U.S. plant and of the large plant in a developing country appears to confirm that some adaptation to the local environment did in fact take place. It cannot be said, however, how much of this adaptation was due to the lower cost of labor and how much was due to the scarcity of maintenance personnel.

The steps and functions defined as crucial seem to be equipped with automated controls more often than the others. In fact if an attempt is made at ranking the potential cost of an error in the control of the various functions listed in this table, this ranking seems to be directly related to the degree of automation.

The large developing country plant had a higher degree of automation than did the two small plants. This large plant and the small privately owned plant are located in areas with the same availability of skilled labor. One explanation of this difference in level of automation is that the large plant is a joint venture between local interests and a large foreign pulp and paper company. Although the foreign participation is a small minority position and the local sponsors manage the firm, the foreign partners had provided expatriate labor during the first few years of operation and technical assistance thereafter. The large firm thus had an access to skills that the small firm lacked. In support of this explanation, after the departure of the foreign technicians, a number of automatic controls were removed or disconnected because of maintenance problems. Another reason for the smaller plant's extensive use of manual controls is the smaller size of its processing units, which makes for easier manual control and therefore reduced risk of errors.

There are no apparent differences in the levels of automation of the small privately owned and the small government-owned plants. This finding contrasts sharply with the earlier findings in the textile industry. The explanation lies in the fact that the designs for both plants came from the same small group of consulting and engineering firms and equipment suppliers that specialize in this field.

Conclusions
and Policy
Recommendations

This inquiry has attempted to settle some controversies about the choice of production technologies in developing countries. At the very least it should end the uncertainty as to how such choices are made in the pulp and paper and the textile industries. Far from being merely theoretical this issue has important policy implications for governments of developing countries, as well as for industrial firms operating in these countries. Although there is wide disagreement about what technology is best suited to a specific environment, the potential rewards from choosing adapted technologies are important: a potential for more rapid economic development and for increased employment and a heightened ability to compete in world markets.

This study addressed the three main issues around which the controversy about technology choice in developing countries has centered:

1. Is there a range of alternative technologies available for the production of a good? If so do these alternative technologies use the factors of production in proportions different enough to make the choice between them a significant issue?

2. What is the role played by production cost minimization in technology choice, assuming that firms face a range of alternative technologies that employs the factors of production in significantly different proportions?

3. Are there other considerations besides or in lieu of production cost minimization that influence a choice of technology? What are these considerations, and does their impact differ according to the type of firm?

These issues were investigated in order to provide answers to some highly controversial questions. One question relates to the impact of foreign direct investment on technology choice in developing countries: is foreign direct investment to be encouraged for its transfer of technologies that are urgently needed for economic development? Or is it to be discouraged because the technologies it transfers are unadapted to developing countries?[1] Another question deals with the effect of government intervention on the relative attractiveness of alternative technologies: is government intervention the best way to promote the adoption of suitable technologies, or is it the source of many of the distortions that lead to the adoption of unadapted ones?[2]

The Scope for Technology Choice

A compilation of the alternative technologies available in the textile and pulp and paper industries as well as an estimation of their input requirements reveals that alternative technologies requiring significantly different quantities of labor and capital are available to perform most processing operations in these industries. The number of such alternatives, however, was found to be limited rather than infinite, as assumed by neoclassical economic theorists. For some processing steps, in fact, there are very few alternatives. Even in those cases where few alternatives are available, the relative quantities of capital and labor they require still differ enough to make the choice of technology a relevant issue in terms of demand for these factors of production.

Such findings are not surprising in the textile industry, where numerous other studies have already reached the same conclusions.[3] They are, however, somewhat more unexpected in the pulp and paper industry. There has been little investigation of the scope for capital-labor substitution in chemical process industries such as pulp and paper. Yet the assumption has usually been that this scope is limited.[4] This apparent contradiction is explained by the different nature of the alternatives that offer capital-labor trade-offs in mechanical as opposed to chemical industries.

Although alternative technologies offering trade-offs between capital and labor usage exist in both industries, the form they take in each of these differs widely. In the textile industry where the transformation process is a relatively simple mechanical one, the alternative technologies are embodied in the main pieces of equipment. In the pulp and paper industry, on the other hand, the transformation of the raw material is achieved through the action of chemicals, heat, and pressure. Because there is little room for direct manual participation in the transformation process, the alternative technologies available in the main pieces of equipment are few. The trade-offs they offer between capital, use of the different chemicals, and energy also tend to overshadow those that may exist between capital and labor; however, the reactions and flows that take place in these processing units can be controlled in a variety of ways, from the manual opening and closing of valves to computerized monitoring and adjustments. As a consequence capital-labor trade-offs in the pulp and paper industry are made in the choice of instrumentation and control equipment rather than in the choice of the processing equipment.

Previous studies evaluating the scope for capital-labor trade-offs in chemical industries focused on processing equipment, as was done for mechanical industries. Whatever conclusions were drawn as to the absence of such trade-offs in chemical industries did not take the control and instrumentation functions into account. Furthermore the spectrum of alternatives considered included only technologies in actual use by the firms studied. Since chemical facilities of the same size tend to choose the same processing technologies (as is confirmed by this study), these previous inquiries identified very few of the alternatives that were actually available.

In trying to explain the adoption of relatively capital-intensive technologies in developing countries, several authors have suggested that labor-intensive technologies require more supervisory and skilled personnel than do capital-intensive ones.[5] This hypothesis has led some authors to argue that capital-intensive technologies are in fact best suited to developing countries.[6] It has rarely been put to the test, however, because the measures of capital or labor intensity used—generally various ratios of capital, labor, and output—could consider only two factors of production. The findings of this study tend to refute this hypothesis.

A comparison of the input requirements of the alternative technologies in the textile and the pulp and paper industries reveals that more capital-intensive technologies require a greater proportion of their labor input in the form of skilled and supervisory workers. In fact a number of more capital-intensive technologies require altogether larger absolute numbers of skilled and supervisory workers than do less capital-intensive ones.

In the textile industry the more labor-intensive technologies require a larger percentage of their capital input in the form of buildings. Since building costs in developing countries mostly consist of payments to local labor while equipment costs take the form of foreign exchange payments, the former are preferable from the country's point of view.

In his study of Kenyan manufacturing firms, Howard Pack pointed to what he called "the substitution between labor and buildings."[7] Since building costs were not included in his estimations of the investment cost of alternative technologies, however, his study did not reach conclusions as to the impact of this larger building cost component on the competitiveness of labor-intensive technologies.

Factor Costs, Production Cost Minimization, and Technology Choice

Neoclassical economic theorists start with the premise that for the production of any given good, there exists an infinite number of technologies combining labor and capital in varying proportions. They then assume that production cost minimization is the only criterion that firms will apply in their choice from among these alternatives. If factor prices are determined by market forces, neoclassical theory shows that this criterion should lead to a choice of technology that combines the factors of production in a ratio equal to that of their availabilities.

There are two highly debated aspects of this theory, apart from the assumption that a spectrum of alternative technologies exists. One is the extent to which firms make use of production cost minimization as a criterion for technology choice. The second is the extent to which factor price distortions explain technology choices that are nonoptimal from the country's point of view. Since the methodology developed for this study allows for the identification of the cost-minimizing technologies from the firm's and from the country's standpoint, an assessment of the role of production cost minimization in a firm's choice of technology and of the impact of factor cost distortions on the optimum is possible.

Important differences were found in the role and application of the production cost minimization criterion in the textile and the pulp and paper industries. In the textile industry chosen technologies are more labor intensive than the technology that is optimal for developed countries' conditions. This indicates that some adaptation to the cost of the factors of production in developing countries has taken place. In about half of the cases where adaptation took place, however, it was not complete. A technology intermediate in capital intensity between the U.S. technology and the technology that would have minimized the firm's production cost was chosen. Therefore while production cost-minimization through capital-labor trade-offs appears to be a factor in textile firms' choice of technology, it is not the only consideration.

This less-than-complete adaptation to the market cost of the factors of production resulted in an increase of, on average, 22 percent of the cost of transformation for these firms. Its impact on factor usage was even more important: choosing the cost-minimizing technology would have reduced overall capital requirements by a third and foreign exchange requirements by half and would have increased employment by 50 percent.

In the pulp and paper industry a very limited but still noticeable amount of adaptation to factor cost takes place. This is borne out by the small differences in mill design that exist between developed and developing countries among plants of the same size. This adaptation takes place only in very specific functions, however. Furthermore with increases in the scale of operation, adaptation decreases more rapidly than would be justified by the economic impact of such changes in scale.

The choice of technology for chemical processing equipment appears to be entirely a function of scale and technical factors. Although a small mill might have a lower capital-labor ratio than a larger one with identical control equipment, this change in labor intensity is a consequence only of changes in scale and would take place regardless of the respective cost of labor and capital. Production cost minimization remains the principal criterion used for the selection of processing equipment technologies in the pulp and paper industry. The minimization of chemicals, power, and steam usage and the maximization of machine efficiency, however, are the crucial factors in the application of this criterion. Trade-offs between capital and labor are considered to be side effects of the optimization effort rather than its main variable, as in the textile industry.

The choice of technology for handling and transfer operations is the most sensitive to differences in factor cost. Whenever technically feasible, labor-intensive technologies are chosen if they are economically competitive. The technical feasibility and economic competitiveness of labor-intensive handling technologies, however, diminish with increases in scale.

Some adaptation to factor cost structure also seems to take place in the choice of control technologies. Yet for some control tasks the most manual alternatives were systematically avoided. Here, too, while much adaptation takes place in mills of small capacity, this adaptation decreases sharply in larger mills. This reduction in the level of adaptation is greater than appears justified by the enhanced competitiveness of the more automated technologies. The juxtaposition in the same mills of labor-intensive control technologies with more capital-intensive ones casts some doubt on whether these choices were only the result of a cost-minimization effort based on capital and labor costs. These findings suggest the existence of some other considerations in the choice of control technologies.

The extent to which factor price distortions can influence technology choice in the pulp and paper industry is mitigated by the limited emphasis on production cost minimization and the minor role that labor prices play in any cost-minimization effort. Such distortions nevertheless can be expected to be important in the textile industry, where production cost minimization bears greatly on technology choice and where capital and labor prices are crucial variables in this effort.

The impact of factor cost distortions was estimated by comparing the technology that minimizes production cost at the market price of the factors of production (market optimum) with the cost-minimizing technology at the social costs (social optimum). The social optimum technology differs from the market optimum technology in slightly fewer than half of the cases studied. Although distortions in the cost of labor, capital, and foreign exchange are important in all the developing countries covered, a shift in optimum does not always take place because of the noncontinuous nature of the spectrum of technology alternatives. In situations where the social and market optima are different, the differences in the employment generation and capital usage of these two technologies are large. Factor price distortions thus have an important economic cost.

A comparison of the technologies chosen with those that would have used the countries' resources in the most economically efficient manner aggregated the effect of partial adaptation by firms and the impact of factor price distortions. This provides a picture of the economic consequences of suboptimal choices whatever the reason for this suboptimality. In the textile industry only half of the potential job creation was achieved, and this was done at a capital cost of approximately a third higher than would have been socially optimal.

Non-Factor-Price Considerations in Technology Choice

Since the technologies chosen are, in a majority of the cases, not the ones that would yield the lowest production cost to the firm, considerations other than production cost minimization influence the choice of technology.

Availability and Cost of Information

The identification of the optimum technology in a specific environment calls for detailed knowledge of the input requirements of alternative technologies and equipment. Yet firms base their analyses on much more limited information, which better covers the technologies at the more capital-intensive end of the spectrum.

In the textile industry detailed information about alternative technologies and equipment designs is available since equipment is standardized and purchased on an off-the-shelf basis. Professional publications and forums, however, tend to emphasize innovations that generally take place at the capital-intensive end of the technology spectrum. Equipment that incorporates the most labor-intensive technologies is often no longer produced in developed countries and is available only from equipment manufacturers in developing countries. Because information tends to flow from developed to developing countries rather than between developing countries, these firms and the equipment they produce are not known to textile manufacturers in other developing countries. These equipment manufacturers are also too small to be able to afford a network of representatives and to engage in promotional efforts.

In the pulp and paper industry the lack of information on alternative technologies and equipment designs is due to the high cost of obtaining information rather than to imperfections in the information flows. In that industry technologies must be adapted to the characteristics of the raw material used by each production unit, requiring that the main pieces of equipment be custom made. The high cost associated with the development of each alternative dictates that the number of alternatives contemplated be kept to a minimum. The selection by a firm of the alternatives to be evaluated is thus based on limited information. The criterion used to assess the potential attractiveness of an alternative is the importance to the mill's overall efficiency of the variable that is manipulated in this alternative. Using that yardstick alternatives whose objective is the use of a larger amount of labor because of its low cost rank well below alternatives that might lead to improvements in machine efficiency, wood yield, or chemical and power consumption.

The reliance on outside organizations for the planning and design of new projects is far greater in the pulp and paper industry than in the textile industry. The experience of the very few organizations with planning and design capabilities for pulp and paper mills is heavily weighted toward the capital-intensive end of the technology spectrum, and so are the designs they proposed. This is not surprising given that all these firms are located in developed countries and that developing countries have so far represented a very small percentage of their market.

Several other studies conclude that unavailability of or limitations in the search for information explain the adoption of capital-intensive technologies. Wells in Indonesia, Morley and Smith in Brazil, and Mason in the Philippines and Mexico found that foreign firms had a high propensity to choose equipment from their home country.[8] This was confirmed by Stobaugh's study of the impact at home of foreign investment by American firms.[9] Wells, and Morley and Smith have found a strong link between equipment origin and capital intensity. Imported equipment was clearly more capital intensive than local equipment. All of these studies, however, investigated industries for which domestically manufactured equipment was available, which is not the case here. Expanding on the conclusions of these previous works, this study shows that the issue is not so much one of imported versus domestic equipment but rather one of country of origin. Instead of purchasing equipment from other developing countries, locally owned firms in developing countries without a local source of equipment turn to developed countries as their source of supply. These local firms then exhibit the same pattern of behavior as do subsidiaries of foreign firms, and this results in the choice of more capital-intensive technologies.[10]

The cost of obtaining information about alternative technologies has also been cited as a reason for a firm's lack of adaptation. This cost is shown to depend on industry characteristics, and is higher for chemical process industries than for mechanical process industries. When information costs are high, firms try to limit the number of alternatives they consider. Taking advantage of a lower cost of labor then ranks low as a reason to select such alternatives.

Minimization of Risk Considerations

Three types of risk considerations influence the choice-of-technology decision: the evaluation of business and political risks, the consideration of risks associated with the utilization of the different factors of production, and the drive to protect the firm's competitive position.

Since business and political risks are taken into account in the pricing of capital, they should not further influence the firm's choice of technology. Foreign-owned firms, however, further indicate a desire to minimize investment cost because of political and business risks.

A concept of risk associated with the use of different factors of production is also apparent. In developing countries the risk associated with the use of machines (the embodiment of capital) is a consequence of the difficulty of obtaining spare parts and adequate technical assistance in case of breakdown. Firms minimize this risk by limiting their choice of technology to simple, common designs and by their self-imposed restriction to well-known suppliers with large service networks. This restriction tends to narrow further the range of alternatives considered and to eliminate some of the smaller suppliers. These smaller suppliers often are those that produce the more labor-intensive technologies because of their lack of research facilities.

The risks associated with the use of labor include strikes and worker unrest, as well as human error in the operation of equipment. The risk of labor unrest encourages firms to limit the size of their work force and therefore to choose more automated technologies when possible at a small cost. Nevertheless foreign-owned firms, which might be expected to be more sensitive to risks associated with labor, do not choose more capital-intensive technologies than do local firms of similar characteristics. This may, however, be the result of a balancing of two opposite factors: the foreign firm's aim of limiting its investment and its preoccupation with the problems of managing a large labor force.

An operator's error or failure to perform his task results in a cost to the firm. This cost varies widely according to the industry, the processing step in which the error occurs, and the specific task to be carried out. The cost of human error is higher in the pulp and paper industry than it is in the textile industry. The pulp and paper industry reacts to this cost by being less sensitive than the textile industry to differences in the relative cost of labor and capital. The risk of human error was often spoken of as the motivating factor in the choice of automatic controls for pulp and paper plants. In both industries, however, the higher cost of human error in the steps of the production process that are crucial in determining the quality of the output or the overall efficiency of the plant explains the higher degree of automation found in these steps. At the other extreme materials handling steps are those whose technology is most readily adapted to take advantage of lower labor costs. In a parallel manner it was found that in a given processing step, technologies that provide automation of processing tasks are adopted more often than technologies that allow for automation of handling tasks. The only other study to have separated handling and processing steps noted the larger employment-creation effect of technology adaptation in the handling steps and the higher propensity of firms to adapt technologies in these steps.[11]

The third type of risk consideration that influences the choice of technology and equipment supplier affects smaller firms or newcomers in an industry. This is the risk inherent in deviating from the technology choices made by the industry leaders. This factor influences the choice of equipment supplier more than the choice of technology. Such imitative behavior is justified by the fact that large orders from the industry leader often prompted the equipment suppliers that received them to establish a local service network. A similar reasoning makes the subsidiaries of foreign firms choose the same equipment suppliers as their home country facilities. In that case it is to take advantage of the relations already established with these suppliers and of the accumulated experience with their equipment.[12]

Competitive pressure is a strong determinant of the amount of attention given to production cost minimization and therefore of the degree of adaptation of the chosen technology. Lack of profit motivation explains the tendency of government-owned firms to base their technology choices on pure engineering criteria. It results in the selection of more capital-intensive equipment than that of their privately owned competitors. Such conclusions were also reached by Williams in his study of the government textile sector in Tanzania.[13]

Firms with a strategy of product differentiation also depart from the general level of capital intensity adopted by other firms. Their choice of technology considers elements other than production cost minimization. The capacity of each technology to further the differentiation of their products clearly predominates here. For this reason firms that differentiate their products on the basis of quality choose more capital-intensive equipment. On the other hand a firm specializing in small orders produced on short notice selected equipment that is more labor intensive than warranted by cost minimization. Several studies, including those by Wells and Yeoman, also found that firms with a strategy of product differentiation, either through quality or through branding, had a higher than average level of capital intensity.[14] No situations were mentioned in these studies where product differentiation led to a lower than average capital intensity.

All of the plants in this study owned by firms from other developing countries were found to have a higher than average level of capital intensity and to have decided on a strategy of product differentiation through quality.[15] This finding, however, is based on a small number of such plants and can only be considered indicative.

Government Policies

Government policies that did not directly affect the cost of the factors of production have had an important effect on the choice of technology. Examples of such policies are the arbitrary allocation of scarce capital whose price is kept too low for demand and supply to balance each other, government policies regarding the local procurement of equipment or the financing terms of imported equipment, and government tax incentives designed to attract investment or encourage the relocation of firms.

Policy Recommendations

The conclusions of this study point to five types of government policies that can be used to promote the adoption of more labor-intensive technologies in developing countries.[16]

Identification and Promotion of Labor-Intensive Industries

This is a well-recognized policy tool for maximizing employment creation at a given level of capital investment. Such a policy is also relatively easy to implement in developing countries since industrial ventures in these countries normally require government approval. Its use, however, has been limited since it conflicts with governments' other objectives of self-sufficiency and industrial base diversification. What this study adds to the existing body of knowledge about such policies is that the identification of the industries to be promoted should be based on an evaluation of the technological alternatives available in each industry. Instead, industries generally have been evaluated on the basis of one capital-labor ratio—a country or worldwide average in most cases.

Identification and Promotion of Types of Firms Using Labor-
Intensive Technologies

In any given industry certain types of firms, differentiated by their
ownership, national origin, or scale of operation, might use more labor-
intensive technologies than others. These types should be identified
and promoted. The existing evidence that would allow such policies
to be developed is still sketchy though. While a strong prejudice has
often existed in developing countries against foreign firms, this study
did not uncover any significant difference in the choices of technology
made by foreign and local firms. The only firms for which there is
evidence of a tendency to select capital-intensive technologies are government owned. Although this might conflict with other government
objectives, if only employment creation is considered, the government
ownership of individual firms should not be promoted in developing
countries.

While small-scale operations, particularly in the pulp and paper industry, were found to be more labor intensive, this higher level of labor
intensity is reached at a cost in terms of efficiency. Therefore, special
incentives to this type of firm do not appear to be appropriate. The
promotion of such firms may in fact result in the use of both more
capital and labor for the production of a given quantity of output.
Overall not enough evidence is yet available to prompt the development
of policies favoring certain types of firms for the purpose of increasing
employment. This is an area where further research could make
substantial contributions.

Dissemination of Information on Labor-Intensive Technological
Alternatives

Government action on this front could yield substantial benefits. In
the textile industry unavailability of information tends to eliminate the
most labor-intensive technologies from the range of alternatives considered. This is a deficiency that can easily be corrected by means of
government intervention. Technology or technical assistance centers
can collect such information, particularly about equipment producers
in other developing countries and the machines they offer, and make
it available to manufacturers. Particular attention should be paid to
staffing such centers with professionals who know the requirements
and criteria of manufacturers. These centers should not only have the

capability to identify and evaluate labor-intensive technologies but should also be in a position to assist smaller equipment manufacturers in providing after-sale service. Such policies should prove effective in promoting labor-intensive alternatives in mechanical industries where equipment is normally standardized.

The problem is different in chemical industries such as pulp and paper because of the made-to-order nature of the industry's basic equipment. At best information can be collected about engineering and consulting firms with experience in developing countries and that offer more adapted designs. Because the cost of information was the main obstacle to the development of adapted designs, government organizations (such as technology centers) can offer to underwrite the cost of developing technological alternatives whose aim is to reduce capital cost and increase employment. Such a policy would be feasible only in industries with a large potential for development in the country, such as pulp and paper in Brazil. In other industries where only one or a very small number of plants can be expected in a country, development costs would be too heavy for that country to bear, and only international organizations or intercountry cooperative agreements would be in the position to implement such a policy.

Manipulation of Factor Prices

Much emphasis has been given in the literature and in economic forums to the efforts that developing countries should make to reduce existing distortions in factor prices and bring these prices more in line with real costs to their economies. There are, however, a myriad of government policies that result in factor price distortions—from minimum wage laws and subsidization of the cost of capital as the most obvious, to accelerated depreciation, tax holidays, and import duties on equipment as more indirect ones. Changing each of these policies would not entail the same costs or yield the same amount of benefits, necessitating some amount of discrimination. Furthermore there is no evidence that the efforts required to disentangle the complex web of policies that affect factor prices—most of which have been developed for the satisfaction of other government objectives—would yield the highest return in terms of employment creation. The reduction of factor price distortions would bring the market optimum closer to the social optimum. For such a shift to have an impact on the technology choices made by firms, however, one must still assume that greater potential production cost savings would cause firms to adopt more labor-intensive technologies. For this assumption to be valid, firms would have to know about these more labor-intensive alternatives. Also noncost considerations should not tip the scale against taking advantage of this opportunity.

Among those actions that can be taken to reduce factor price distortions, some will be more effective than others. Changes in tax rates and tax laws will not have much impact on the choice of technology made by firms. Indications are that the impact of taxes is not taken into consideration when alternative technologies are evaluated. Changes in the cost of capital, on the other hand, seem to have an important impact on technology choice. Not only was this found to be an important factor in the financial justification of alternative technologies, but it was also shown to affect several risk considerations. The repeal of minimum wage laws seems difficult to justify from a political point of view. The granting of labor subsidies, on the other hand, would pose tremendous administrative problems.

Modification of Non-Factor-Price Considerations

Government policies can influence some of the non-factor-price considerations that play a role in the firms' choice of production technologies, in order to bring the technologies chosen closer to the cost-minimizing technologies at market prices. Competitive pressures on the firm are an important determinant of its propensity to minimize production cost through the adoption of labor-intensive technologies. By reducing the amount of protection given to firms, by granting production licenses in a more liberal manner, and by preventing the formation of cartels, governments can increase the competitive pressure on firms. High taxes on advertising expenses would also tend to make strategies of product differentiation through branding less attractive. Governments can design policies dealing with the domestic production and import of capital goods with a view to favoring equipment embodying labor-intensive technologies and ensuring them an adequate and timely supply of spare parts. So far such policies have been designed solely on the basis of balance-of-payments considerations and have had the opposite effect on technology choice.

Finally whatever the policies adopted, governments can promote the use of labor-intensive technologies by making the evaluation of the technology proposed a major element of their analysis of projects. The granting of incentives and licenses can then be linked to the adoption of technologies that are suited to the country's environment. To implement such a policy, governments need a good knowledge of the available alternatives and a methodology for comparing the economic impact of these alternatives if they were to be adopted in a specific project. Definitions of the available alternative technologies and of their requirements such as those developed in this study for the textile and the pulp and paper industries can be provided by a technology center. A methodology to compare these alternatives from both the firm's and the country's point of view in the framework of a specific project was proposed in this study.

Appendix A

Main Characteristics of the Companies Studied

Table A.1
Textile Plants

Company[a]	Country	Ownership[b]	Activities[c]	Number of Shifts[d]	Strategy[e]	Exports[f]
1	Colombia	Local (GP)	S, W, F	3		30%
2	Colombia	Local (GP)	S, W, F	3		25
3	Colombia	Local (GP)	S, W, F	3		35
4	Brazil (south)	Maj. foreign (LDC)	S, W, F	3	Prod. diff.	15
5	Brazil (northeast)	Maj. foreign (LDC)	S, W, F	3	Prod. diff.	10
6	Philippines	Local (Fam.)	S, W, F	3		15
7	Philippines	Local (GP)	S, W, F	3		20
8	Philippines	Local (GP)	S, W, F	3		10
9	Philippines	Local (Fam.)	S, W, F	3		15
10	Philippines	Local (Fam.)	S, W, F	3	Prod. diff.	0
11	Indonesia	Maj. foreign (LDC)	S	3	Prod. diff.	0
12	Indonesia	Maj. foreign (DC)	S, W, F	4		0
13	Indonesia	Maj. foreign (DC)	S, W, F	4		0

Table A.1 (continued)

Company[a]	Country	Ownership[b]	Activities[c]	Number of Shifts[d]	Strategy[e]	Exports[f]
14	Indonesia	Local (Govt)	S, W	4		0
15	Indonesia	Local (Govt)	S, W	3		0
16	Indonesia	Maj. foreign (DC)	S, W, F	4		0
17	Japan	Local (GP)	S, W, F			
18	Japan	Local (GP)	S, W, F			
19	United States	Local (GP)	S, W, F	3		

a. These numbers are used in the other appendixes to identify the companies.

b. Local = More than 95 percent of shares controlled by nationals (GP = general public; Fam. = family owned; Govt = government owned). Min. foreign = More than 5 percent but less than 50 percent of shares controlled by foreign nationals. Maj. foreign = More than 50 percent but less than 95 percent of shares controlled by foreign nationals (LDC = foreign nationals from a developing country, DC = foreign nationals from a developed country). Foreign = More than 95 percent of shares controlled by foreign nationals.

c. S = spinning. W = weaving. F = finishing.

d. A plant with three shifts operates 24 hours a day, 5.5 to 6 days a week—therefore 6,600 hours to 7,200 hours per year. A plant manned by four shifts operates 24 hours a day, 7 days a week, and up to 52 weeks a year—therefore 8,400 to 8,700 hours per year.

e. Only firms that considered themselves to have a strategy of product differentiation are identified in this column.

f. Percentage of sales of cloth revenues accounted for by direct exports of the company. When the company had several plants this export figure is for the company as a whole rather than the particular plant studied. Cloth exported in the form of finished garments, whether made by the company studied or by other local firms, is not included in these figures.

Table A.2
Pulp and Paper Plants

Company	Country	Ownership[a]	Size[b]	Activities[c]	Exports[d]
1	Colombia	Maj. Foreign (DC)	Medium	Pu, Pa	0%
2	Colombia	Local (GP)	Small	Pu	0
3	Brazil (south)	Maj. foreign (DC)	Medium	Pu, R, Pa	0
4	Brazil (south)	Maj. foreign (DC)	Medium-Large[e]	Pu, B, R, Pa	0
5	Brazil (south)	Maj. foreign (DC)	Large	Pu, R	100
6	Brazil (south)	Local (GP)	Large	Pu, B, R, Pa	0
7	Brazil (south)	Local (GP)	Medium	Pu, B, R, Pa	0
8	Philippines	Local (Fam.)	Small	Pu, R, Pa	0
9	Philippines	Min. foreign (DC)	Small	Pu, B, R, Pa	0
10	Philippines	Min. foreign (DC)	Medium	Pu, B, R, Pa	10
11	Indonesia	Local (Govt)	Small	Pu, B, R, Pa	0
12	Indonesia	Local (Govt)	Small	Pu, B, Pa	0
13	United States	Local (GP)	Large	Pu, B, R, Pa	
14	United States	Local (GP)	Large	Pu, B, R, Pa	

a. See note b to table A.1.

b. Small = Mill of less than 100 tons per day of air-dried pulp production capacity. Medium = Mill of between 100 tons per day and 400 tons per day of air-dried pulp production capacity. Large = mill of more than 400 tons per day of air-dried pulp production capacity.

c. Pu = Pulp making. B = Bleaching of pulp. R = Chemical recovery of pulping chemicals. Pa = Papermaking.

d. Exports of paper and paperboard produced by these plants in the form of containers or wrappings for other goods produced by the country (fruits, for example) are not included in these figures.

e. The expansion project studied is to increase mill capacity from medium to large according to the above definition of size categories.

Appendix B

Function and Principle of Operation of Each Processing Step in the Industries Studied

Textile: The Short Fiber Spinning and Weaving Process

The Opening Room

Three steps are performed in the opening room: plucking (also called breaking or opening), cleaning, and scutching (also called picking). Their purpose is to mix the fiber coming from different bales, to break up the lumps of compressed fiber contained in the bales, and to remove foreign matter that has not been eliminated during the ginning process. Because of small variations from one bale to another in the characteristics of cotton, the mixing of raw cotton from different bales is necessary to assure the uniform blend required for efficient spinning and weaving. These three steps are performed continuously as the cotton is automatically transported from one machine to another by moving belt or air flow.

Plucking Small amounts of fiber are taken alternately, either manually or automatically, from several bales and fed into the continuous opening line by a mechanism that regulates the flow and further blends the various tufts of cotton.

Cleaning The cotton then goes through a sequence of machines (step cleaners, condensers, breakers, reserve chambers, etc.) which increases the mixing by accumulation in chambers, further loosens the lumps of cotton by beating, and removes foreign matter through tumbling and air flow. The number and arrangement of these machines depend upon the cleanliness and uniformity of the cotton bought by the mill and the quality of the end product sought. All these machines operate automatically and require labor only for monitoring and maintenance.

Scutching At the end of this line a machine or set of machines, called scutchers or finisher-pickers, prepare the cotton for delivery to the next processing step. Their role is to regulate the flow of fiber and then either form these fibers into a lap (roll) to be carried to the carding machines or distribute the fibers directly to these machines through an air-flow system.

The Spinning Shed

The purpose of the processing steps that make up the spinning shed, is, after a final cleaning of the cotton, to further disentangle the fibers, to align them in parallel configuration, to condense them into a tiny sliver, and finally to twist this sliver to increase its strength. To obtain a yarn of very high quality, the shorter fibers will be removed in an extra step called combing. This step is not required in the production of ordinary yarn. The cotton fibers that entered the spinning shed in the form of a clean, opened, and unstructured mass will leave it in the form of bobbins (called cheeses or cones) of yarn that can be used for weaving, knitting, or sewing and are commonly traded between firms and countries.

Carding   Carding further cleanses and disentangles the fibers and changes the bulk, raw stock into a sliver, a loose, rope-like strand of fibers about the size of a man's thumb. No twisting is applied to the fibers in the carding frame. The sliver is soft, smooth, and fluffy, and the fibers in it are clean and parallel.

Drawing   In this step, draft (pulling) is applied to the strand of fibers through the action of a set of rollers rotating at different speeds. This causes the fibers to be drawn among themselves to a longer and straighter finished length. Since this drafting causes the diameter of the strand to decrease, several strands are brought together at the feeding end of the frame (doublings). Depending upon the quality and the fineness of the yarn to be manufactured, the stock is run through drawing frames between one and six times (generally two or three).

Combing   For the production of very fine yarns, a step called combing is inserted between the first and second drawings. This precise operation completes the cleansing of the fibers and removes the short, undesirable fibers while the choice, long fibers are assembled to become a silk-like strand. Before the combing frames, a sliver lap or ribbon lap frame needs to be added to prepare the stock for feeding into the combing frames. Combing is, however, rarely found in textile mills in developing countries.

Roving   The stock coming out of the last drawing is still in the form of a sliver contained in cans, and although this sliver has been subjected to drafting actions, it still has the diameter of a thumb because of the doublings. In the roving frames, more draft will be applied to the cotton sliver. For the first time in the process, it will also be given some twist. Since there are no doublings on the roving frame, the strand will emerge much thinner, about the size of the lead in a pencil, and will be wound onto a bobbin or roving spindle.

Spinning   This step, which gives its name to the whole process, produces the yarn in its final form. As in the roving step, draft and twist are applied to the sliver without doubling it up. The result is that this strand, now called "yarn," comes out of the spinning frames much thinner and more break-resistant. It is wound on small bobbins called spindles.

Winding   The yarn comes out of the spinning frames wound onto small bobbins, and it still contains some spinning irregularities that might cause breakages in the weaving operation. The purpose of the winding step is to wind the yarn onto large bobbins, either cylindrical or conical, depending on its projected use, and to eliminate these irregularities. While being rewound on large packages, the yarn is subjected to a slight tension and goes through an "epuration system" that induces the yarn to rupture at weak as well as excessively thick points. This break is repaired after the irregularities are eliminated.

The Preparatory Section

The yarn enters this section in the form of cylindrical or cone-shaped bobbins either directly from the spinning shed or from a yarn-finishing department where it has been dyed or treated. In this section the yarn will be prepared for the weaving stage. The large number of threads that are to form the basis of the cloth, the warp, will be wound on a loom, or warp beam, while the yarn to be used as filling will be wound in packages appropriate for the insertion method of the looms used. For this reason the preparatory section is divided into two subsections: the warp yarn section and the filling yarn section.

Warp Yarn   In this section three operations are performed sequentially: warping, sizing (or slashing), and drawing-in. *Warping* consists of winding a large number (300–600) of strands of yarn onto a warp beam. This is a delicate operation since each yarn must be wound under the same tension and the number or yarn breakages has to be kept low to minimize the number of machine stoppages. These beams are then taken to a sizing, or slashing, machine. *Sizing* consists of the coating of warp yarns with starch in order to increase their resistance to abrasion during the weaving operation. On the feeding end of the sizing machine, several warp beams are unwound simultaneously in order to increase the number of strands per inch to the required level. These strands are then dipped into a starch solution, dried by passing on large heated cylinders and rewound on the beam that will be placed on the loom. Before this beam is put on the loom, a last operation called *drawing-in* takes place. In this operation each thread from the warp beam is pulled through an eyelet on one of the frames that, once on the loom, will command the opening of the warp for the insertion of the filling yarn.

Weft Yarn   In the weft section the yarn to be used as filling is wound into a package that can be fed into the insertion mechanism of the loom. For shuttle looms, where the filling is inserted by a shuttle, the weft yarn must be wound onto very small bobbins called pirns, or cops, which can be placed in the shuttle. This operation is called *pirn winding*.

Some modern looms do not use a shuttle for the insertion of the weft yarn. These "shuttleless looms" can take weft yarn in the form of the large conical bobbins that were produced at the winding step. Consequently, shuttleless looms do not require any preparation of the weft yarn, and this section does not exist in plants that use shuttleless looms.

The Weaving Shed

Although only one processing step is performed in this section, it is a very important part of the mill since it generally accounts for about a third of the capital cost and of the employment generated by a balanced spinning-weaving mill. The inputs of the weaving step are warp and weft yarn ready to be used by the looms, the output is gray cloth that can go either to a finishing department after inspection for defects, or can be sold outside. The weaving process consists of inserting the filling yarn between alternating sets of warp yarn. This operation binds these yarns together and, depending upon the way these sets of yarn are alternated, gives to the finished product a certain feel, look, or property.

Although gray cloth is commonly traded between firms and countries, it is rarely used in that form by the final consumer. It is generally subjected to a finishing process that includes at least washing and bleaching. These operations and others such as dying, printing, and Sanforizing take place in the finishing department of the mill or at the facilities of specialized finishers.

Pulp and Paper: Sulfate Process Pulping and Papermaking

The Wood Yard

Debarking   The first step in the transformation of tree logs into paper is debarking. This procedure can be performed either as part of the forestry operations before the shipping of logs to the mill or in the wood yard of the mill. After the bark is stripped from the logs, it is usually compressed and fed to the boilers for the generation of steam and power.

Chipping   Then comes the chipping step where the logs are cut into small pieces about two inches long and one-half inch thick so that the wood can absorb the pulping chemicals more easily.

Chip Storage   Since the wood yard generally works on a one or two shift basis while the rest of the pulp and paper mill works 24 hours a day, a chip storage step normally concludes the wood yard operations.

The Pulp Mill

The objective of the pulping process is to separate the cellulose fibers from which the paper is made, from the noncellulosic element, the lignin, that binds these fibers together. This can be done by mechanical action, producing what is called "ground-wood pulp" of which newsprint is made, or by chemical means, to obtain a "chemical pulp." A combination of both processes—called a semimechanical process— may also be employed. Here the lignin is first softened by a limited chemical action, the fibers then being separated from the lignin by means of abrasion. The quality of the paper that will be obtained from a given type of wood depends upon the gentleness and the thoroughness with which the lignin is removed. The less damaged the cellulose fibers are after the pulping process and the less lignin that remains in the pulp, the higher the price the pulp or the paper will command. A parallel increase in production costs takes place, however, because expensive chemicals rather than mechanical action have to be used and a smaller quantity of pulp is obtained from a given quantity of wood.

The sulfate pulping process studied in this document is a chemical pulping process that uses a solution of sodium hydroxide, sodium carbonate, and sodium sulfide to dissolve the lignin. It is a process that yields one of the highest quality pulps obtainable from a given quality of wood.

Digesting   In the digesting step, the wood chips are impregnated with the solution of pulping chemicals—the pulping liquor—under high temperature and pressure. The combined action of chemicals, heat, and pressure breaks down the lignin.

Blow tanks   Once most of the lignin has been degraded or dissolved, the wood, which still has the physical form of chips, is expelled into a blow tank where a rapid drop in pressure breaks up these chips and reduces them to pulp.

Defiberizing   Next, the pulp goes through a series of defiberizers or refiners where, through slight mechanical action, the fibers are further disentangled and separated and knots of fibers are opened.

Washing   The next processing step consists of a series of three to five washers. Here, clean water is pumped through the pulp in order to wash away the dissolved lignin and the pulping chemicals. The chemical and lignin solution pumped out of the washers—called weak liquor—may either be disposed of or diverted into a recovery system whose purpose is to extract and recycle the chemicals.

Screening   The now clean pulp goes through a screening step. Here, lumps of fibers still bound up by undissolved lignin are separated and sent back to the digesters. When leaving the screening step, the pulp slurry contains only 5 percent solid matter (cellulose fibers). The rest is water. The slurry may either be directed into a bleaching process or be sent to the stock preparation department without bleaching.

Thickening   Before entering the stock preparation department, however, and regardless of whether it has undergone bleaching or not, the slurry material is generally stored. The purpose of this intermediate storage is to reduce the impact on the paper mill of possible variations in the rate of pulp production. Because storage of a pulp slurry containing only 5 percent solid matter would be extremely expensive, its concentration in cellulose fibers is first enhanced by means of a thickening process in which water is removed.

High-density storage   The concentrated pulp slurry, now with a consistency of approximately 14 percent solid matter, is then piped into high-density storage tanks.

The Stock Preparation Department

In this department the pulp, which comes either from the plant's own high-density storage tanks or is purchased from outside suppliers in the form of "pulp sheets," is prepared for the paper machine.

Slushing   If the pulp has been purchased outside and is in the form of pulp sheets (dried pulp), it first has to go through a slushing step in order to be brought back to liquid form.

Beating   Once the pulp slurry has been brought back to a consistency of 3.5 percent solid matter, it undergoes a beating operation. Its purpose is to open the cellulose fibers to facilitate their bonding at the paper-making stage, thus yielding a more tear-resistant paper.

Refining   Following beating comes another refining step that breaks up any remaining fibrous lumps and produces a very uniform slurry.

Blending   Finally, at the blending stage, the different types of pulp required for the production of a specific type of paper are mixed and special-purpose additives, such as resin and starch, are added.

The Paper Mill

The paper mill houses two types of equipment: the paper machines and the slitter rewinders.

Papermaking   The paper machine distributes a measured, uniform amount of pulp slurry over a moving wire mesh and then, through the actions of gravity, suction, pressure, and heat, removes the water from this slurry. The result will be a sheet of paper that is wound on reels at the other end of the machine. Although the paper machining process is simple, the paper machine represents a major part of the equipment cost of a balanced sulfate process pulp and paper mill.

A paper machine comprises six sections: The head box, which meters out a uniform, measured amount of liquid pulp; the wire, which is a sort of moving wire mesh through which water escapes, first through the action of gravity, then through suction; the press section where the pulp, after leaving the wire, is pressed through felt cylinders; the drying section, where the sheet of paper circulates around large cylinders heated through internal circulation of steam; the calender rolls where the sheet is given a uniform thickness through the pressure of polished steel rolls; and the winding section where the paper is wound on a pope reel.

Slitting-rewinding   The slitter-rewinders, of which there is one at the end of each paper machine, rewind the reel of paper produced by the paper machine, cutting it lengthwise so as to reproduce narrower and smaller reels of paper.

The Finishing Department, the Recovery System, and the Bleaching Department

Since these departments were excluded from the scope of this study, their processing steps will not be described here. The bleaching department and the finishing department were omitted because of the large number of alternative processes that can be designed depending upon the whiteness of the paper and the paper format that are demanded by the market. The recovery system was excluded because of the complexity of the process and the changes it undergoes depending upon the availability and cost of the various pulping chemicals.

Detailed
Description
of Alternative
Technologies
in the Textile
Industry

Alternative Technologies for Plucking

Cotton or polyester is fed into the opening and cleaning line through a plucker. Because of small differences in the characteristics of cotton, or to a lesser extent polyester, coming from different bales, several bales have to be mixed to obtain a uniform raw material. It is for this mixing of the different bales that alternative technologies are available.

Technology 1: Up to twelve opened bales are laid out in front of the apron of the plucker. The operator picks a small amount of raw material from each of these bales in turn and places it on the moving belt that feeds the plucker.

Technology 2: Several bales (generally six or eight) are placed in the plucker, which automatically takes small amounts of raw material from each of these bales in turn. Because of a greater regularity in the amount being taken from each bale, fewer bales (generally half the number) have to be mixed than in technology 1.

Technology 3: Same technology as number 2 except that additional bales are put in reserve positions, or more than one bale can be put in each of the positions so that when one bale is finished, another one takes its place automatically. Such a unit has to be loaded only every eight to twelve hours.

Alternative Technologies for Scutching

At the end of the opening and cleaning line, a machine called the finisher picker, or scutcher, rolls the opened processed cotton into a lap, which is then presented to the carding machines.

Technology 1: When the lap has reached a certain size, the scutcher is manually stopped, the lap is removed, its axis is changed, and it is weighed, coded, and stored (all manually) before being manually carried to the carding machines.

Technology 2: Same as technology 1 except that the stoppage of the scutcher at a predetermined size of lap, removal of the lap, and restarting of the scutcher on a new lap is automatic. The change of axis, weighing, cooling, storing, and transport remain manual.

Technology 3: All operations are automatic up to the storage of the lap. Only the transport of the lap from storage to the carding machine is done manually.

Technology 4: Same as technology 3 except that instead of being automatically stored and then manually transferred to carding machines, laps are automatically loaded on a chain conveyor system, which takes them to the carding machines and automatically loads them on whichever card needs a new lap.

Technology 5: This technology is completely different from the preceding ones in that the scutcher is eliminated and the opened and cleaned cotton, instead of being rolled into a lap for transfer to the carding machines, is sent directly to these machines by a flow of air through ducts. An automatic distribution system directs the necessary amount of cotton to the chute feeding each of the carding machines.

Alternative Technologies for Carding

Although their basic principle is always the same, carding machines differ in the speed at which they operate, which determines for a given amount of production the number of units that have to be monitored, cleaned, serviced, and maintained; the size of the cans in which the carded raw material goes, which determines the number of can changes per unit of time; and the degree of automation of the card cleaning and can changing operation.

Technology 1: Low-speed card (5 to 10 kilograms per hour). No enclosure to contain dust and totally manual waste collection. Small carded raw material cans in which the sliver coming out of the card can be placed without the assistance of an automatic coiler and manual can change.

Technology 2: Medium-speed card (15 to 20 kg per hour). The card is enclosed, and the dust and waste are automatically collected and stored in a waste compartment by a pneumatic system. It is then manually removed from each card's waste compartment. As in technology 1, the cans are small and manually changed when full.

Technology 3: Same as technology 2 except that the carded raw material is placed into large cans by a power coiling system. The cans are still manually changed when full.

Technology 4: High-speed cards (more than 20 kg per hour). Enclosure and waste collection system centralized at the machine level as in technology 3. Large cans with power coiling system and manual can change also, as in technology 3.

Technology 5: Same as technology 4 except that the can is automatically replaced by an empty one when full. Since the change is immediate, the carding machine does not have to stop, which results in an increase in machine efficiency.

Technology 6: Same as technology 5 except that the waste and dust, instead of being automatically collected in a waste compartment in the carding machine and manually removed from there, go automatically by a pneumatic system to a centralized waste sorting unit for the whole spinning mill.

Technology 7: Same as technology 6 except that the sliver coming out of the carding machine is not coiled into a can; instead it goes directly into the next processing machine (a drawing frame) where it joins slivers coming from other cards. This means that the transfer from the carding machine to the drawing frame is completely automatic.

Alternative Technologies for Drawing

As for carding, the main technological alternatives are based on the speed at which the drawing frames operate and therefore their processing capacity per unit of time. Alternatives also exist in the degree of automation of the feeding of the frames and changing of the cans in which the processed material goes.

Technology 1: Low-speed processing heads (150 to 300 meters per minute), two deliveries per frame. The drawing frame is fed from cans manually transferred from the carding machines and positioned. The cans in which the sliver delivered by the drawing frames is coiled are changed manually when full.

Technology 2: High-speed processing heads (300 to 400 m/mn), two deliveries per frame. Rest as in technology 1.

Technology 3: Same as technology 2 except that the cans in which the processed fibers are coiled are changed automatically.

Technology 4: Very high-speed processing heads (500 m/mn), only one delivery per drawing frame. The carded fibers are fed into the drawing frames directly from the cards (see carding technology 5) in ribbon form, rather than in cans, and the delivery can is changed automatically.

Alternative Technologies for Winding

Alternative technologies in the winding step are based on different degrees of automation of: the knotting of the yarn and restarting of the winding after a yarn breakage or when a new spindle or package is started; the removal of the spinning spindles once the yarn has been unwound from them and the feeding of full ones; and the removal of the yarn package when it has reached a predetermined size or weight and the feeding of a new core to start a new package.

Technology 1: All operations are manual. The yarn is knotted manually, empty spindles are replaced by full spindles manually, and full packages are replaced by empty cores, also manually.

Technology 2: The knotting is done automatically by a traveling knotter. The empty spindles are automatically removed and replaced by a full spindle that has been manually placed in a reserve position corresponding to each unwinding head. The packages are changed manually when full.

Technology 3: The knotting is done automatically by a knotter, which services a smaller number of winding heads than in technology 2. The empty spindles are automatically removed and replaced by full ones that have been manually placed in a reserve magazine corresponding to each winding head or to a set of these winding heads. Since the reserve magazine holds a number of spindles (in technology 2 it holds only one), it requires less attention from the operator and leads to greater efficiency. The packages are changed manually when full.

Technology 4: Same as technology 3 except that the full packages are removed automatically and replaced by empty cores automatically as well.

Technology 5: Same as technology 3 except that a separate independent machine prepares the full spindles for feeding into the reserve magazine. Because of this preparation, they can be put in the magazine much faster, and a small automatic attachment on the winding head is able to find the extremity of the yarn without the operator's positioning it. As in technology 3, the removal of full packages and feeding of empty cores is done manually.

Technology 6: Same as technology 5 except that the removal of full packages and feeding of empty cores is done automatically, as in technology 4.

Technology 7: The basic unit is the same as in technology 3 except that the full spindles, instead of coming from a reserve magazine corresponding to each winding head and in which the spindles have to be individually positioned by hand, come from a bulk bin at the end of the winding frame in which they are thrown without preparation. Knotting is automatic and changing of packages manual, as in technology 3.

Technology 8: Same as technology 7 except that the removal of full packages and feeding of empty cores is done automatically.

Technology 9: Same as technology 8 except that the full spindles, instead of being transported manually from the spinning frames to the winding frames and dumped into the bulk bins, are automatically transferred between the two steps, and the empty spindles are automatically returned to the spinning frames. This system is normally associated with automatic doffing features at the spinning frames.

Alternative Technologies for Pirn Winding

This processing step exists only when shuttle looms are used. The pirn-winding operation is similar to the winding operation except that in this case the yarn is rewound from the winding packages onto small bobbins (or cops) to be inserted in the looms' shuttles. Also since no cleaning of the yarn takes place in this step, yarn breakages are infrequent. The alternative technologies in this step are based on different levels of automation in the feeding of the cops, which, since they are very small, fill up rapidly and must be changed often. None of the equipment manufactured features automatic knotting or automatic change of the package since shuttleless looms would always be more economical than shuttle looms and pirn winders equipped with such advanced automatic features.

Technology 1: Manual removal of filled cops and feeding of empty ones.

Technology 2: Automatic removal of filled cops and feeding of empty ones from a reserve stack in which they are individually positioned by hand.

Technology 3: Automatic removal of filled cops and feeding of empty ones from a bulk bin, serving a large number of pirn winding heads, in which empty cops are dumped without positioning or preparation.

Technology 4: Unifil. The pirn winding is done on each loom instead of on a separate machine as an independent processing step. An attachment to each loom receives the winding packages and rewinds the yarn onto a cop, which then automatically replaces the shuttle cop when it is empty. The empty cop is then automatically refilled to be ready for a new change.

Alternative Technologies for Weaving

In weaving the warp yarn is held by the loom, and the weft yarn is inserted across the warp in an interlacing fashion. The weft is inserted (pulled across the warp) either by means of a shuttle, which carries it back and forth across the warp, or, for shuttleless looms, by other devices. The shuttle contains a spool of wound yarn, or cop, which unwinds the weft as the shuttle is moved across the warp. A measure of technical efficiency of a loom type is given by the number of insertions per minute. The average rate of insertions per minute, for standard cloth width, measures the speed of the loom.

Technology 1: Hand loom: 60 insertions per minute; manual operation; shuttle inserted manually.

Technology 2: Power, shuttle: 120 insertions per minute. Shuttle inserted automatically; when cop inside the shuttle is empty, the loom stops; to resume, the shuttle containing the empty cop is replaced manually by a shuttle containing a full one.

Technology 3: Power, shuttle, automatic shuttle change: 150 insertions per minute. Power operation, with the shuttle inserted automatically. When the cop is empty, a new shuttle with a fully wound cop replaces the old shuttle automatically. Workers load full cops into shuttles and stack them onto a frame on the loom for automatic feeding.

Technology 4: Power, shuttle, automatic cop change, side picking, mechanical control: 175 insertions per minute. Power operation; shuttle inserted automatically. When cop is empty, a full wound cop automatically replaces it in the shuttle, which itself is not replaced. The mechanism for inserting the shuttle (picking) is moved by a lever action from the side (side picking). This operation is controlled mechanically.

Technology 5: Power, shuttle, automatic cop change, parallel picking, mechanical control: 200 insertions per minute. Power operation; shuttle inserted automatically. When cop is empty, a fully wound cop automatically replaces it in the shuttle, which itself is not replaced. The mechanism for inserting the shuttle (picking) is moved by a shoe pulling parallel to the shuttle insertion direction (parallel picking). This operation is controlled mechanically.

Technology 6: Power, shuttle, automatic cop change, parallel picking, electronic control: 240 insertions per minute. Power operation; shuttle inserted automatically. When the cop is empty, a fully wound cop automatically replaces it in the shuttle, which itself is not replaced. The mechanism for inserting the shuttle (picking) is moved by a shoe pulling parallel to the shuttle insertion direction (parallel picking). This operation is controlled electronically.

Technology 7: Power, shuttleless, rigid rapier: 260 insertions per minute. Power operation. Shuttleless loom utilizing telescopic arms (rigid rapier) that pull the weft across the warp. The weft is wound onto large bobbins fixed to the side of the loom.

Technology 8: Power, shuttleless, flexible rapier; 270 insertions per minute. Power operation. Shuttleless loom utilizing a flexible steel ribbon (flexible rapier) that pulls the weft across the warp. The weft is wound onto large bobbins fixed to the side of the loom.

Technology 9: Power, shuttleless, projectile: 260×2 insertions per minute (loom of double width). Power operation. Shuttleless loom utilizing a projectile that is propelled across the loom and carries the weft across the warp. The weft is wound onto large bobbins fixed to the side of the loom.

Technology 10: Power, shuttleless, air jet: 450 insertions per minute. Power operation. Shuttleless loom where the weft is pulled across the warp by a jet of air rather than by mechanical devices. The weft is wound onto large bobbins fixed to the side of the loom; commercial sales of this type of loom have begun only recently.

Technology 11: Power, shuttleless, multiphase: 700 insertions per minute. Power operation. Shuttleless loom where a number of projectiles are inserted in close sequence so that several weft yarns are woven simultaneously, though not in phase. The projectiles are not propelled from one end of the loom to the other but rather are pushed forward across the warp by mechanical fingers appearing between the warp yarns in a wavelike motion. This loom is still in development stages.

Appendix D

Comparison of the Cost of
Transformation and Factor
Requirements of Social
Optimum, Market
Optimum, and Chosen
Technologies for the
Textile Firms Studied, by
Processing Step and
Company (in percentage)

	Company																		
	1	2	3	4	5	6	7	8	9	10	11	12	13	14	15	16	17	18	19
	Colombia			Brazil		Philippines					Indonesia						Japan		U.S.

Plucking

Propensity to adapt

	1	2	3	4	5	6	7	8	9	10	11	12	13	14	15	16	17	18	19
At social market prices	100	100	100	0	0	100	100	100	100	100	100	100	100	100	100	100	100	100	100
At market prices	100	49	56	0	0	100	92	100	100	93	100	100	100	100	100	100	100	100	100
Cost due to distortion	0	37	37	40	46	0	40	0	0	40	0	0	0	0	0	0	0	0	0

Employment created

	1	2	3	4	5	6	7	8	9	10	11	12	13	14	15	16	17	18	19
Versus social optimum	100	100	100	32	32	100	100	100	100	100	100	100	100	100	100	100	100	100	89
Versus market optimum	100	275	275	89	88	100	275	100	100	275	100	100	100	100	100	100	100	100	89
Loss due to distortion	0	64	64	64	64	0	64	0	0	64	0	0	0	0	0	0	0	0	0

Employment, supervisory, skilled

	1	2	3	4	5	6	7	8	9	10	11	12	13	14	15	16	17	18	19
Versus social optimum	100	100	100	81	81	100	100	100	100	100	100	100	100	100	100	100	100	100	116

Versus market optimum	100	141	141	115	113	100	143	100	141	100	100	100	100	100	100	116
Loss due to distortion	0	29	29	29	28	0	30	0	29	0	0	0	0	0	0	0
Employment, semiskilled, unskilled																
Versus social optimum	100	100	100	25	25	100	100	100	100	100	100	100	100	100	100	80
Versus market optimum	100	319	321	80	80	100	319	100	320	100	100	100	100	100	100	80
Loss due to distortion	0	69	69	69	69	0	69	0	69	0	0	0	0	0	0	0
Capital requirement																
Versus social optimum	100	100	100	146	145	100	100	100	100	100	100	100	100	100	100	120
Versus market optimum	100	79	79	121	121	100	80	100	79	100	100	100	100	100	100	120
Increase due to distortion	0	26	26	21	20	0	26	0	26	0	0	0	0	0	0	0
Equipment requirement																
Versus social optimum	100	100	100	188	188	100	100	100	100	100	100	100	100	100	100	134

Appendix D (continued)

	Company																		
	1	2	3	4	5	6	7	8	9	10	11	12	13	14	15	16	17	18	19
	Colombia			Brazil		Philippines					Indonesia						Japan		U.S.
Versus market optimum	100	72	72	134	134	100	72	100	100	72	100	100	100	100	100	100	100	100	134
Increase due to distortion	0	40	40	40	40	0	40	0	0	40	0	0	0	0	0	0	0	0	0
Buildings requirement																			
Versus social optimum	100	100	100	100	100	100	100	100	100	100	100	100	100	100	100	100	100	100	100
Versus market optimum	100	100	100	100	100	100	100	100	100	100	100	100	100	100	100	100	100	100	100
Increase due to distortion	0	0	0	0	0	0	0	0	0	0	0	0	0	0	0	0	0	0	0
Foreign exchange requirement																			
Versus social optimum	100	100	100	1463	1429	100	100	100	100	100	100	100	100	100	100	100	0	0	0
Versus market optimum	100	74	74	131	131	100	75	100	100	74	100	100	100	100	100	100	0	0	0

Scutching

Increase due to distortion																
0	35	35	1015	990	0	34	0	0	34	0	0	0	0	0	0	0
Propensity to adapt																
At social prices																
100	100	100	0	0	69	32	69	100	0	64	100	0	32	100	0	0
At market prices [a]																
100		100	0	0	43	3	26	100	0	61	100	0	(13)	100	0	0
Cost due to distortion																
0	100	100	0	0	0	0	0	0	0	0	0	0	0	0	0	0
Employment created																
Versus social optimum																
100	100	1191	61	8	86	68	86	100	8	85	100	7	68	100	564	820
Versus market optimum																
100	168	1210	100	8	86	68	86	100	100	85	100	7	68	100	564	820
Loss due to distortion																
0	92	92	39	0	0	0	0	0	0	0	0	0	0	0	0	0
Employment, supervisory, skilled																
Versus social optimum																
100	100	163	61	60	102	120	102	100	60	97	100	54	120	100	198	198
Versus market optimum																
100	168	168	100	60	102	120	102	100	120	97	100	54	120	100	198	198
Loss due to distortion																
0	39	40	39	0	0	0	0	0	0	0	0	0	0	0	0	0

Appendix D (continued)

	Company																		
	Colombia			Brazil		Philippines					Indonesia						Japan		U.S.
	1	2	3	4	5	6	7	8	9	10	11	12	13	14	15	16	17	18	19
Employment, semiskilled, unskilled																			
Versus social optimum	100	100	100	1	1	100	84	61	84	100	1	84	100	1	61	100	100	3138	5045
Versus market optimum	100	7982	7900	100	1	100	84	61	84	100	1	84	100	1	61	100	100	3138	5045
Loss due to distortion	0	99	99	99	0	0	0	0	0	0	0	0	0	0	0	0	0	0	0
Capital requirement																			
Versus social optimum	100	100	100	171	171	100	119	147	119	100	171	117	100	170	141	100	100	94	83
Versus market optimum	100	55	55	100	171	100	119	147	119	100	171	117	100	170	141	100	100	94	83
Increase due to distortion	0	81	81	71	0	0	0	0	0	0	0	0	0	0	0	0	0	0	0
Equipment requirement																			
Versus social optimum	100	100	100	197	197	100	122	155	122	100	197	122	100	197	155	100	100	91	78

Versus market optimum	100	51	51	100	197	100	122	155	122	100	197	122	100	197	155	100	100	91	78
Increase due to distortion	0	97	97	97	0	0	0	0	0	0	0	0	0	0	0	0	0	0	0
Buildings requirement																			
Versus social optimum	100	100	100	74	74	100	100	93	100	100	74	100	100	74	93	100	100	125	125
Versus market optimum	100	135	135	100	74	100	100	93	100	100	74	100	100	74	93	100	100	125	125
Increase due to distortion	0	(26)	(26)	(26)	0	0	0	0	0	0	0	0	0	0	0	0	0	0	0
Foreign exchange requirement																			
Versus social optimum	100	100	100	371	371	100	121	152	121	100	185	119	100	185	149	100	0	0	0
Versus market optimum	100	52	52	100	371	100	121	152	121	100	185	119	100	185	149	100	0	0	0
Increase due to distortion	0	93	93	271	0	0	0	0	0	0	0	0	0	0	0	0	0	0	0
Carding																			
Propensity to adapt																			
At social prices	53	88	9	0	(61)	76	0	54	9	100	0	47	75	47	47	100	(147)	(128)	0

Appendix D (continued)

	Company																		
	1	2	3	4	5	6	7	8	9	10	11	12	13	14	15	16	17	18	19
	Colombia			Brazil		Philippines					Indonesia						Japan		U.S.
At market prices	57	365	1	0	(80)	169	0	53	8	100	0	49	134	40	44	100	(145)	(128)	0
Cost due to distortion	0	0	0	0	0	0	0	0	C	0	0	0	0	0	0	0	0	0	0
Employment created																			
Versus social optimum	71	275	52	41	26	275	41	71	52	100	41	70	276	71	71	100	19	26	63
Versus market optimum	71	275	52	41	26	275	41	71	52	100	41	70	276	71	71	100	19	26	63
Loss due to distortion	0	0	0	0	0	0	0	0	0	0	0	0	0	0	0	0	0	0	0
Employment, supervisory, skilled																			
Versus social optimum	91	205	58	60	53	205	60	91	58	100	59	87	206	89	91	100	53	54	89
Versus market optimum	91	205	58	60	53	205	60	91	58	100	59	87	206	89	91	100	53	54	89
Loss due to distortion	0	0	0	0	0	0	0	0	0	0	0	0	0	0	0	0	0	0	0

Employment, semiskilled, unskilled

Versus social optimum	66	293	50	37	19	293	37	66	50	100	37	66	292	67	66	100	11	19	52
Versus market optimum	66	293	50	37	19	293	37	66	50	100	37	66	292	67	66	100	11	19	52
Loss due to distortion	0	0	0	0	0	0	0	0	0	0	0	0	0	0	0	0	0	0	0

Capital requirement

Versus social optimum	122	178	150	147	170	178	153	122	151	100	147	122	180	122	122	100	175	171	115
Versus market optimum	122	178	150	147	170	178	153	122	151	100	147	122	180	122	122	100	175	171	115
Increase due to distortion	0	0	0	0	0	0	0	0	0	0	0	0	0	0	0	0	0	0	0

Equipment requirement

Versus social optimum	123	174	161	164	192	174	164	123	161	100	164	123	174	123	123	100	201	192	118
Versus market optimum	123	174	161	164	192	174	164	123	161	100	164	123	174	123	123	100	201	192	118
Increase due to distortion	0	0	0	0	0	0	0	0	0	0	0	0	0	0	0	0	0	0	0

Appendix D (continued)

	Company																		
	1	2	3	4	5	6	7	8	9	10	11	12	13	14	15	16	17	18	19
	Colombia			Brazil		Philippines					Indonesia						Japan		U.S.
Buildings requirement																			
Versus social optimum	116	205	74	83	83	205	83	116	74	100	83	116	205	116	116	100	68	83	100
Versus market optimum	116	205	74	83	83	205	83	116	74	100	83	116	205	116	116	100	68	83	100
Increase due to distortion	0	0	0	0	0	0	0	0	0	0	0	0	0	0	0	0	0	0	0
Foreign exchange requirement																			
Versus social optimum	123	175	158	161	188	175	160	123	158	100	156	123	177	123	123	100	0	0	0
Versus market optimum	123	175	158	161	188	175	160	123	158	100	156	123	177	123	123	100	0	0	0
Increase due to distortion	0	0	0	0	0	0	0	0	0	0	0	0	0	0	0	0	0	0	0
Drawing																			
Propensity to adapt																			
At social prices	94	100	94	100	97	100	93	100	100	100	97	69	97	97	69	97	0	0	0

At market prices	98	95	100	100	100	100	100	100	100	99	100	64	100	100	72	100	0	0	0
Cost due to distortion	0	6	6	0	3	0	7	0	0	7	3	3	3	3	3	3	0	0	0
Employment created																			
Versus social optimum	90	100	90	100	90	100	90	100	100	100	90	80	90	90	81	90	51	51	177
Versus market optimum	90	111	100	100	100	100	100	100	100	111	100	89	100	100	90	100	51	51	177
Loss due to distortion	0	10	10	0	10	0	10	0	0	10	10	10	10	10	10	10	0	0	0
Employment, supervisory, skilled																			
Versus social optimum	87	100	88	100	86	100	87	100	100	100	87	83	86	86	87	86	111	110	90
Versus market optimum	87	115	100	100	100	100	100	100	100	115	100	98	100	100	100	100	111	110	90
Loss due to distortion	0	13	12	0	14	0	13	0	0	13	13	15	14	14	13	14	0	0	0
Employment, semiskilled, unskilled																			
Versus social optimum	91	100	91	100	91	100	91	100	100	100	91	80	91	91	80	91	40	40	219
Versus market optimum	91	110	100	100	100	100	100	100	100	110	100	88	100	100	88	100	40	40	219

Appendix D (continued)

	Company																		
	1	2	3	4	5	6	7	8	9	10	11	12	13	14	15	16	17	18	19
	Colombia			Brazil		Philippines					Indonesia							Japan		U.S.
Loss due to distortion	0	9	9	0	9	0	9	0	0	9	9	10	9	9	9	9	0	0	0
Capital requirement																			
Versus social optimum	105	100	105	100	101	100	105	100	100	100	101	118	101	101	119	101	134	134	89
Versus market optimum	105	95	100	100	100	100	100	100	100	95	100	117	100	100	117	100	134	134	89
Increase due to distortion	0	5	5	0	1	0	5	0	0	5	1	1	1	1	1	1	0	0	0
Equipment requirement																			
Versus social optimum	111	100	111	100	111	100	111	100	100	100	111	131	111	111	131	111	151	151	79
Versus market optimum	111	90	100	100	100	100	100	100	100	90	100	119	100	100	119	100	151	151	79
Increase due to distortion	0	11	11	0	11	0	11	0	0	11	11	11	11	11	11	11	0	0	0

Buildings requirement

Versus social optimum	73	100	73	100	73	100	73	100	100	100	73	82	73	73	82	73	51	51	220
Versus market optimum	100	137	100	100	100	100	100	100	100	137	100	113	100	100	113	100	51	51	220
Increase due to distortion	0	(27)	(27)	0	(27)	0	(27)	0	0	(27)	(27)	(27)	(27)	(27)	(27)	(27)	0	0	0

Foreign exchange requirement

Versus social optimum	109	100	109	100	115	100	109	100	100	100	106	125	106	106	125	106	0	0	0
Versus market optimum	109	92	100	100	100	100	100	100	100	92	100	118	100	100	118	100	0	0	0
Increase due to distortion	0	9	9	0	15	0	9	0	0	9	6	6	6	6	6	6	0	0	0

Winding

Propensity to adapt

At social prices	46	79	46	47	41	100	100	41	68	100	100	38	100	100	38	100	0	0	100
At market prices	78	94	100	71	65	100	89	58	100	82	100	52	100	100	52	100	0	0	100
Cost due to distortion	21	54	54	40	19	0	32	0	32	32	0	26	0	0	26	0	0	0	0

Appendix D (continued)

	Company																		
	1	2	3	4	5	6	7	8	9	10	11	12	13	14	15	16	17	18	19
	Colombia			Brazil		Philippines					Indonesia						Japan		U.S.
Employment created																			
Versus social optimum	24	45	24	23	23	100	100	24	45	100	100	100	100	100	24	100	51	51	100
Versus market optimum	53	188	100	93	50	100	221	24	100	221	100	100	100	100	53	100	51	51	100
Loss due to distortion	55	76	76	76	55	0	55	0	55	55	0	0	0	0	55	0	0	0	0
Employment, supervisory, skilled																			
Versus social optimum	53	68	53	56	56	100	100	53	68	100	100	100	100	100	53	100	107	107	100
Versus market optimum	78	127	100	106	83	100	148	53	100	147	100	100	100	100	78	100	107	107	100
Loss due to distortion	32	47	47	47	32	0	32	0	32	32	0	0	0	0	32	0	0	0	0
Employment, semiskilled, unskilled																			
Versus social optimum	22	44	22	20	20	100	100	22	44	100	100	100	100	100	22	100	41	41	100

Versus market optimum	50	199	100	91	46	100	229	22	100	229	100	100	100	100	50	100	41	41	100
Loss due to distortion	56	78	78	78	56	0	56	0	56	56	0	0	0	0	56	0	0	0	0
Capital requirement																			
Versus social optimum	234	196	235	251	251	100	100	336	281	100	100	100	100	100	308	100	145	145	100
Versus market optimum	120	83	100	111	135	100	36	336	100	36	100	100	100	100	121	100	145	145	100
Increase due to distortion	95	135	135	126	86	0	178	0	181	180	0	0	0	0	154	0	0	0	0
Equipment requirement																			
Versus social optimum	250	211	250	283	283	100	100	379	320	100	100	100	100	100	379	100	148	148	100
Versus market optimum	118	84	100	113	134	100	31	379	100	31	100	100	100	100	118	100	148	148	100
Increase due to distortion	111	150	150	150	111	0	220	0	220	220	0	0	0	0	220	0	0	0	0
Buildings requirement																			
Versus social optimum	122	79	122	116	116	100	100	122	79	100	100	100	100	100	122	100	121	121	100

Appendix D (continued)

	Company																		
	1	2	3	4	5	6	7	8	9	10	11	12	13	14	15	16	17	18	19
	Colombia			Brazil		Philippines					Indonesia						Japan		U.S.
Versus market optimum	154	65	100	95	147	100	127	122	100	127	100	100	100	100	154	100	121	121	100
Increase due to distortion	(21)	22	22	22	(21)	0	(21)	0	(21)	(21)	0	0	0	0	(21)	0	0	0	0
Foreign exchange requirement																			
Versus social optimum	246	207	246	763	759	100	100	364	307	100	100	100	100	100	345	100	0	0	0
Versus market optimum	119	84	100	130	156	100	33	364	100	33	100	100	100	100	120	100	0	0	0
Increase due to distortion	107	146	146	488	388	206	206	0	207	206	0	0	0	0	188	0	0	0	0
Pirn Winding																			
Propensity to adapt																			
At social prices	100	100	100	(118)	(104)	100	100	100	0	100	0	0	100	0	0	100			
At market prices	100	a	a	a	a	100	100	100	0	a	0	0	100	0	0	100			
Cost due to distortion	0	100	100	100	100	0	0	0	0	100	0	0	0	0	0	0			

Employment created

Versus social optimum	100	100	100	110	110	100	100	88	100	88	100	88	88	100
Versus market optimum	100	113	113	125	125	100	100	88	113	88	100	88	88	100
Loss due to distortion	0	12	12	12	12	0	0	0	12	0	0	0	0	0

Employment, supervisory, skilled

Versus social optimum	100	100	100	192	191	100	100	122	100	122	100	119	122	100
Versus market optimum	100	82	82	157	156	100	100	122	82	122	100	119	122	100
Loss due to distortion	0	(22)	(22)	(22)	(22)	0	0	0	(22)	0	0	0	0	0

Employment, semiskilled, unskilled

Versus social optimum	100	100	100	105	105	100	100	86	100	86	100	86	86	100
Versus market optimum	100	116	116	122	122	100	100	86	116	86	100	86	86	100
Loss due to distortion	0	14	14	14	14	0	0	0	14	0	0	0	0	0

Appendix D (continued)

	Company																		
	1	2	3	4	5	6	7	8	9	10	11	12	13	14	15	16	17	18	19
	Colombia			Brazil		Philippines					Indonesia						Japan		U.S.
Capital requirement																			
Versus social optimum	100	100	100	254	254	100	100	100	116	100		116	100	116	116	100			
Versus market optimum	100	86	86	220	219	100	100	100	116	86		116	100	116	116	100			
Increase due to distortion	0	16	16	16	16	0	0	0	0	16		0	0	0	0	0			
Equipment requirement																			
Versus social optimum	100	100	100	293	293	100	100	100	116	100		116	100	116	116	100			
Versus market optimum	100	86	86	253	253	100	100	100	116	86		116	100	116	116	100			
Increase due to distortion	0	16	16	16	16	0	0	0	0	16		0	0	0	0	0			
Buildings requirement																			
Versus social optimum	100	100	100	0	0	100	100	100	115	100		115	100	115	115	100			

Versus market optimum	100	87	87	0	0	100	100	100	115	87	115	100	115	115	100	115	100
Increase due to distortion	0	15	15	15	15	0	0	0	0	15	0	0	0	0	0	0	0
Foreign exchange requirement																	
Versus social optimum	100	86	100	907	906	100	100	100	116	100	116	100	116	116	100	116	100
Versus market optimum	100	86	86	598	598	100	100	116	116	86	116	100	116	116	100	116	100
Increase due to distortion	0	16	16	52	52	0	0	0	0	16	0	0	0	0	0	0	0
Weaving																	
Propensity to adapt																	
At social prices	56	56	56	28	28	56	(15)	55	56	55	84	85	57	85	84	(63)	100
At market prices	60	62	63	21	25	60	(22)	59	59	62	88	89	58	100	94	(63)	100
Cost due to distortion	0	9	9	2	7	0	0	0	0	18	0	0	16	15	0	0	0
Employment created																	
Versus social optimum	57	57	56	50	57	57	36	57	61	57	63	60	62	60	57	41	52

Appendix D (continued)

	Company																		
	1	2	3	4	5	6	7	8	9	10	11	12	13	14	15	16	17	18	19
	Colombia			Brazil		Philippines					Indonesia						Japan		U.S.
Versus market optimum	57	91	91	79	85	57	36	57	61	93		63	60	100	100	57	41	52	100
Loss due to distortion	0	38	39	37	33	0	0	0	0	39		0	0	38	40	0	0	0	0
Employment, supervisory, skilled																			
Versus social optimum	76	75	74	58	82	75	70	76	83	76		90	84	85	85	76	42	66	100
Versus market optimum	76	85	85	65	82	75	70	76	83	89		90	84	100	100	76	42	66	100
Loss due to distortion	0	11	13	11	0	0	0	0	0	14		0	0	15	15	0	0	0	0
Employment, semiskilled, unskilled																			
Versus social optimum	54	53	52	48	53	53	30	53	56	53		58	56	59	56	54	41	48	100
Versus market optimum	54	93	93	83	86	53	30	53	56	95		58	56	100	100	54	41	48	100
Loss due to distortion	0	43	44	42	38	0	0	0	0	44		0	0	41	44	0	0	0	0

Capital requirement																		
Versus social optimum	190	193	193	219	217	194	344	193	194	193	130	131	168	130	130	212	237	100
Versus market optimum	190	136	136	166	165	194	344	193	194	136	130	131	129	100	130	212	237	100
Increase due to distortion	0	41	41	32	31	0	0	0	0	41	0	0	30	30	0	0	0	0
Equipment requirement																		
Versus social optimum	247	247	247	348	348	247	468	247	247	247	164	164	247	164	164	261	305	100
Versus market optimum	247	150	150	212	212	247	468	247	247	150	164	164	150	100	164	261	305	100
Increase due to distortion	0	64	64	64	64	0	0	0	0	64	0	0	64	64	0	0	0	0
Buildings requirement																		
Versus social optimum	82	82	82	69	69	82	106	82	82	82	94	94	82	94	94	109	96	100
Versus market optimum	82	88	88	74	74	82	106	82	82	88	94	94	88	100	94	109	96	100
Increase due to distortion	0	(6)	(6)	(6)	(6)	0	0	0	0	(6)	0	0	(6)	(6)	0	0	0	0

Appendix D (continued)

	Company																		
	1	2	3	4	5	6	7	8	9	10	11	12	13	14	15	16	17	18	19
	Colombia			Brazil		Philippines					Indonesia						Japan		U.S.
Foreign exchange requirement																			
Versus social optimum	227	229	229	316	315	226	419	226	226	226		145	145	202	145	145	0	0	0
Versus market optimum	227	488	488	969	962	226	419	226	225	145		145	145	139	100	145	0	0	0
Increase due to distortion	0	(53)	(53)	(67)	(67)	0	0	0	0	55		0	0	45	45	0	0	0	0

Interpretation of propensity-to-adapt ratios: 0 = Optimum technology was chosen. 0–99 = Technology chosen results in a transformation cost lower than if the U.S. technology had been chosen but higher than the optimum technology. 100 = U.S. technology was chosen. Absolute value above 100 = Technology chosen results in a transformation cost larger than if the U.S. technology had been chosen. By convention a positive sign indicates that this technology chosen is more labor-intensive than the optimum technology; a negative sign indicates that the technology chosen is more capital-intensive than U.S. technology.

a. = Value impossible to compute since the denominator of the fraction is zero.

Appendix E

Assumptions and Limitations of the Model and Sources of Data

Underlying Assumptions and Limitations

Exclusion of Duties and Corporate Profit Taxes

The data and methodology used in this study to identify the optimum technologies made such optima independent of the rates of import duties on equipment and of corporate taxes. The use of equipment manufacturers as the source of equipment prices prevented consideration of import duties, while basing the comparisons between technologies on transformation costs rather than on after-tax discounted returns eliminated the impact of profit taxes on such comparisons. Ideally both the level of import duties and the rates of corporate taxes should influence the relative attractiveness of alternative technologies.

The exclusion of duties from the model should not have had any consequences since none of the firms studied had to pay import duties on equipment. Indonesia and the Philippines do not produce any textile or pulp and paper equipment, and all firms in these countries are routinely exempted from duties on imported equipment of any type. In the Philippines this duty exemption is conditional upon the firm's commitment to export part of its output, a commitment more of principle than of substance that all the Philippine firms studied made. Colombia manufactures only one type of loom (simple automatic cop change) and has the same duty exemption rules as the Philippines. There again all of the firms studied were exempted after accepting an export target. Brazil, on the other hand, manufactures a wide variety of textile equipment, mostly under joint-venture or licensing agreements with developed countries' firms. The rules in Brazil are that only the import of equipment whose equivalent is not manufactured locally can be exempted from duty, and duty rates are such that the import of equipment that has not been exempted is not economical. The manufacture of textile equipment, however, developed in Brazil only during the 1970s, and the strict enforcement of these laws is even more recent. The two Brazilian companies studied were exempted from import duties on equipment for the processing steps studied and were required to purchase domestically produced equipment only for processing steps, such as sizing, which were not included in this study. It can therefore be safely said that the exclusion of import duties from this study did not bias its results.

The same cannot be said of the exclusion of corporate taxes from the model. Although most of the companies studied were granted profit tax exemptions for the first two to five years of the life of their projects, these tax holiday periods were much shorter than the normal depreciation period. Since payments to labor can be deducted from taxable income while, among the payments to capital, interest but not loan repayment and dividends can be deducted from the tax base, the higher the tax rate, the higher should be the incentive to choose labor-intensive technologies. (A highly simplified demonstration of this statement is the following: the higher the tax rate, the larger the amount of before-tax profits needed to ensure the required return to one unit of invested capital. Therefore more units of labor must be saved to justify the use of one additional unit of capital.) Therefore the omission of the impact of corporate profit taxes from the analysis may have slightly biased the determination of the market optimum toward more capital intensity. It should not have biased the determination of the social optimum since, in social cost-benefit terms, taxes are internal transfers and not real costs to the economy. The impact of such an omission, however, would have been extremely small, if at all noticeable. Taxation only influences the profitability of alternative technologies after the end of the tax-exempt period, and whatever differential impact it has must then be discounted to year zero. The fact that none of the companies interviewed mentioned tax rates as being a factor in its choice of technology and none included tax computation in its evaluation of the advantages of alternative technologies appears to confirm the limited impact of taxation on the relative attractiveness of alternative technologies. Similar conclusions about the limited influence of tax rates on the choice of technology were reached by Louis T. Wells (1972) in his study of the choice of technology by a sample of Indonesian firms. Although tax rates do not seem to have influenced the choice of technology, they might have had an impact on other aspects of the project analysis, including the decision to invest.

Economic Life of Machinery and Buildings

Normal year cost of transformation evaluations should include a charge for equipment and building usage equivalent to a depreciation of these assets over their economic life. Through the use of such a method, a distinction can be made between equipment of different sturdiness, since these will have different economic lives and therefore a different percentage of their cost to be written off every year. Neither equipment manufacturers nor textile producers, however, could associate economic lives of varying length with equipment of different technologies. Although they could point to differences in the longevity of equipment embodying the same technology but produced by different equipment manufacturers, they could not do so for equipment of different technologies. They considered maintenance quality and unforeseeable technological changes to be the main determinants of the economic life of equipment, whatever the technology embodied in this equipment. In practice the equipment manufacturers and the textile producers visited were found to use standard depreciation periods for equipment and buildings when comparing different equipment or technologies instead of attempting an assessment of the economic life of each alternative.

In this study it was therefore decided to use a standard depreciation period of ten years for all types of equipment and of twenty years for buildings in all countries. These standard depreciation periods are those generally used by the industry.

Machine Efficiency

The method used to compute the number of units of machinery of each technology needed to produce a given quantity of output assumes that the same level of machine efficiency will be reached by a production facility whatever the technology used. In this study two sets of machines embodying different technologies are considered equivalent if their transformation capacities are equal. This definition of equivalency therefore assumes that a given plant should be able to obtain the same quantity of output from two sets of machines of different technology but of similar production capacity.

Although there are no objective grounds for making such an assumption, it is difficult if not impossible to avoid. Only full-scale tests can give an indication of the machine efficiency that can be reached using a specific technology in a given environment. The cost and time involved in making such tests are so substantial that textile companies never attempt them. Lacking such data these firms make the same assumption as the one used in this study for their choice-of-technology decisions.

An attempt was made to reduce the impact of such an assumption by taking into account technology-induced changes in machine efficiency in the evaluation of the equivalence coefficients. For example, when an operation is performed manually instead of automatically, it can be expected that the machine will have to wait to receive the operator's attention while the automatic process would have been activated immediately. In such cases the average waiting time at a given manning level was estimated on the basis of the experience of a number of firms and taken into account in the evaluation of the processing capacity of the manual alternative.

Estimation of Labor Efficiency

The evaluation of the manning requirements of each alternative technology was based on the equipment manufacturer's recommendations. Although slightly optimistic these recommended figures were considered by textile manufacturers to be realistic and representative of the labor requirements of a mill operating at top efficiency. When computing the manning requirements of an alternative technology for a specific mill, the equipment manufacturer's recommended figures for that technology were multiplied by a labor efficiency coefficient, computed to represent the relative efficiency of the labor force of this mill as compared to the top labor efficiency assumed in the base figures.

The labor efficiency coefficient was estimated by comparing the actual manning figures of the plant for a few specific tasks with the manning figures recommended by the manufacturers of the machines used to perform these tasks. The tasks for which this comparison was made were chosen so as to be representative of the range of skills and functions needed in a textile mill.

The use of a unique, firm-specific, labor efficiency coefficient for all skill levels and all alternative technologies makes the underlying assumption that labor efficiency is not a function of the labor intensity or skill requirements of the technology used. If such an assumption had any bearing on the results of this study, it would have favored the more capital-intensive technologies. These technologies generally use, as shown in chapter 2, a mix of labor more heavily weighted toward the higher skills, while the managers interviewed were of the opinion that labor efficiency in developing countries varies inversely with the level of skill required to perform a task.

Preventive Versus Corrective Maintenance

The cost of transformation estimates include the cost of preventive maintenance as well as the cost of parts that have to be changed because of normal wear. They do not include provisions for the cost of corrective maintenance. Under normal operation, meaning operation by a well-trained work force and under strict adherence to preventive maintenance schedules, the amount and cost of corrective maintenance needed should be minimal, limited to the odd accident whose likelihood and cost are difficult to forecast. Since the estimates of manpower and spare parts requirements for preventive maintenance included in this study's transformation cost estimates are based on meticulous maintenance schedules, likely corrective maintenance costs can be considered to be negligible.

Not uncommonly firms neglect preventive maintenance and rely on corrective maintenance when breakdowns occur. This study's underlying assumption would then be that the manpower and spare parts required to perform such corrective maintenance are equivalent to the requirements of an adequate preventive maintenance schedule.

Evaluation of Raw Materials Wastage and of Costs Associated with Off-Quality Products

Raw material losses fall into two categories. The first is the loss in raw material weight resulting from the elimination of foreign matter and very short fibers from the cotton. Since this loss is a function only of the quality of the raw material bought and of the end product sought, it should be the same whatever the processing technology used. It therefore does not need to be taken into account in the comparison of alternative technologies. The second results from equipment and workers' imprecisions and errors and therefore should be a function of both the technology used and the skill level of the work force. Given the complexity and the amount of data required to evaluate these relationships with any degree of reliability, it was assumed that raw materials wastage and the off-quality products rate were the same for all alternative technologies.

In light of the information collected in this study and of the discussions held with textile company managers, this assumption seems reasonable. More capital-intensive machines are generally considered to function more precisely than less capital-intensive ones and thus give lower rates of wastage and off-quality production. In order to perform at these higher levels of efficiency, however, they require a quality of maintenance and tuning that is difficult to reach in developing countries. As a consequence it was found that capital-intensive machines tend to work further from their technical optimum than more labor-intensive ones and thus in practice yield comparable rates of wastage and off-quality production.

Omission of Working Capital Needs

Working capital requirements were not included in the capital cost of the alternative technologies. If raw material usage is assumed to be the same for all alternatives, working capital requirements should differ only by the amount of provisions needed for the payment of salaries and by the cost of the inventory of spare parts. In developed countries labor-intensive technologies are generally assumed to require a larger working capital than capital-intensive ones because of the larger amount of salaries and wages to be paid. If such an assumption was to hold true for the developing countries' facilities studied, the omission of working capital needs from capital requirements should have biased the results in favor of the more labor-intensive technologies.

The difference between the working capital requirements of labor-intensive and capital-intensive technologies, however, is likely to be small in developing countries. While provisions for the payment of salaries and wages tend to be smaller in developing countries because of the lower cost of manpower, spare parts inventories tend to be larger and more costly because of distance from the equipment manufacturers and transportation costs. Such inventory costs also tend to increase with the degree of capital intensity since it was found that spare parts requirements are roughly proportional to machine cost and therefore larger in absolute amount for capital-intensive machinery.

Work in progress and finished goods inventories should not change according to the degree of capital intensity of the machinery for a plant that produces a small variety of finished products. On the other hand for a plant that produces a wide range of products and therefore has short production runs, work in process and finished goods inventories should be smaller when labor-intensive technologies are used. This is a result of the greater scheduling flexibility that stems from the smaller capacity of each unit, and therefore the larger number of units installed for a given volume of production.

Use of Average Cost of Capital

The cost of the increase or decrease in capital requirements resulting from the adoption of one technology over another should be assessed through the use of the marginal cost of capital of the firm. The additional capital required for the installation of a more capital-intensive technology probably would have been obtained at a cost above the present average cost of capital for the firm. The reduction in capital requirement resulting from the adoption of a more labor-intensive technology, on the other hand, would have resulted in a reduction of this average cost of capital. The unavailability of the data needed to compute a marginal cost of capital made it necessary to use the average cost of capital in this model.

The use of an average cost of capital rather than that of a marginal cost should have narrowed the differences in the cost of transformation of alternative technologies. It should not, however, have had any impact on the ranking of these technologies in terms of their cost of transformation.

Sources and Characteristics of Data Used

The data that were used to make the cost of transformation computations, their sources, and the cost elements that were included in the computations are shown in table 3.1.

Equipment Data

Most of the data on equipment that served as the basis for the definition of alternative technologies came from equipment manufacturers. The characteristics of each piece of equipment studied, including its price, were obtained through visits to these manufacturers conducted between

December 1975 and March 1978. Since equipment prices were relatively stable over this period, the specific date at which a manufacturer was interviewed is not thought to have introduced any bias in the results. The prices of equipment that were collected were "f.o.b. zero" prices. This means an f.o.b. European port for European manufacturers, East Coast or West Coast port for American manufacturers, and Japanese port for Japanese manufacturers, including packing for sea shipment and all attachments necessary for normal operation of the equipment. The "f.o.b. zero" price, however, excludes any special features that might be required by the customer, as well as any discounts or special rebates that may have resulted from specific negotiations.

The equipment prices collected differ from the actual cost to the company and therefore should have been reduced by the amount of discounts made by the manufacturer and increased by the cost of sea shipment, insurance, unloading-clearing, land transport, and erection in the country of destination. Interviews with textile firms revealed that the discounts made by equipment manufacturers depended on the size of the order and the state of the equipment market at the time of the purchase rather than on the equipment manufacturer itself or on the type of equipment purchased. Transportation and erection costs were also found to be roughly proportional to the cost of the equipment and were of a magnitude comparable to the rebate usually offered by equipment manufacturers—that is, between 5 and 10 percent of equipment cost. Taken together these two omissions therefore should not introduce any noticeable error or bias in the transformation cost comparisons of alternative technologies for a given firm.

Production Facilities Data

Data on the production facilities include the cost of the different factors of production and other firm characteristics such as the number of shifts or gangs and number of operating hours per year, the technologies chosen, and the number of machines of each technology operating in each processing step. The values collected for these different variables were those at the time of the visits to the textile firms: June and July 1975 for the South American firms and March and April 1976 for the Asian firms.

Although these production facilities data and the equipment data are from the same time period, both sets of data are for a later period than the one in which the choices of technology studied were made.

These choices of technology were made between 1970 and 1973 and therefore were based on the values prevailing at that time for these variables. The period 1970–1975 was characterized by high inflation rates, both for equipment costs and for wages, in the world as a whole as well as in the countries of the sample. These costs did not always evolve in the same way, however. The direction and magnitude of the cost changes during those years depended on the country, the year, and often the type of skill or equipment involved. The impact of the time lag between the technology choice decision and the data collection period on the results of the study is difficult to pinpoint. Yet no evidence was found in the countries and firms examined that the relative price of the factors or the conditions surrounding the choice had changed significantly between these two dates. This impression was confirmed by the textile firms' managers interviewed.

Market prices of the factors of production were collected during the visits to the textile firms. These market prices are firm specific. They are the total cost to a given firm of using one unit of each factor of production considered. Labor prices, for example, are the total costs to the firm of employing one worker of a given skill level. They include fringe benefits, allocation of overtime pay, and taxes paid on salaries, in addition to the actual wage paid to the worker. Power cost, when the power is generated by the firm, includes depreciation and financial costs of the generating facility. The cost of capital includes the borrowing taxes that in some countries must be paid on financial costs. The cost of construction includes the cost of air-conditioning and humidifying equipment allocated on a per-square-meter basis as well as the cost of ducting and electrical equipment. The price of land is not included in building costs since the acreage of land bought or allocated by the government was generally not a precise function of the surface to be built up and therefore should not have been influenced by the choice of production technologies.

Country Data: Social Prices

The link between the market price of the factors of production and the availability of these factors is often considered to break down in developing countries. Government regulations and market interventions aimed at achieving specific economic and social goals are often singled out as the most important causes of such a breakdown. Examples of such government interventions are minimum wage laws that artificially increase the price of unskilled labor, subsidized interest rates, coupled with arbitrary capital allocation mechanisms, fixed exchange rates that are maintained through the use of export incentives on one hand, and duties and quotas on the other.

In such cases an attempt can be made to estimate what should have been the cost of the factors of production had there not been any distortions in the economy. Such prices, called social prices, are those that would lead a rational (cost-minimizing) decision maker to use the factors of production according to their availability and that would therefore prevent any underutilization or shortage of these factors. The optimum technology determined on the basis of these social prices of the factors of production, called the social optimum, is the technology that would have minimized the cost to the country, as opposed to the cost to the company, of producing these goods.

The estimation of a set of shadow prices is a methodologically complex and technically arduous task and was considered beyond the scope of this research. Therefore sets of shadow prices derived through the use of identical methodologies and on the basis of consistent hypotheses for each of the countries studied were sought. These sets of shadow prices were derived from information published by the World Bank and from discussions with World Bank staff. It should be noted, however, that there is no unique and universally accepted methodology for estimating shadow prices and that, even when using a given methodology, different and equally justifiable hypotheses can yield somewhat different results. The shadow prices used in this study are listed in table 3.2. A brief description of the way in which they were derived is given below in order to allow for a critical review of the figures used.

The social cost of supervisory and skilled labor was considered equal to the market cost of these factors since in the countries studied these factors are relatively scarce, and market forces are allowed to determine their cost. The social cost of semiskilled and unskilled labor was taken to be equal to the marginal return on semiskilled agricultural labor for two reasons: the additions to the industrial work force in the countries studied normally come from the agricultural sector and it is the semi-skilled agricultural workers who will tend to move to the cities and be absorbed by the industrial sector after some time. (Semiskilled agricultural workers are defined as workers who have had some limited exposure to modern agricultural methods such as the use of fertilizers, pesticides, or selected seeds as opposed to pure traditional agriculture.) The social cost of semiskilled workers was considered to be the same as that of unskilled workers since most semiskilled workers are recruited as unskilled and are trained on the job. The labor efficiency figures used in the social cost computations were for each country the highest of the labor efficiency figures observed in the production facilities of that country. This figure was selected under the assumption that such an efficiency could be considered an attainable social objective.

The shadow cost of capital was taken to be the marginal economic return of additional investment made in the country considered. The social cost of power was taken as the marginal cost of increased power generation in the country. Although construction costs include a large amount of semiskilled and unskilled labor whose shadow cost should be lower than its market cost, it was impossible to estimate the share of this factor. The social cost of construction in a country was therefore taken as the lowest market construction cost encountered in the firms studied in that country. The foreign exchange component of construction costs, which includes such factors as imported structures and air-conditioning and humidifying equipment, could be defined for each country of the sample.

To correct for distortions in the valuation of the national currency of the countries studied, a shadow foreign exchange factor was used. This adjustment factor is the ratio of the equilibrium exchange rate to the prevailing exchange rate. The equilibrium exchange rate between the national currency and a reference foreign currency, the U.S. dollar, was defined as the exchange rate that would bring autonomous financial flows into equilibrium. Since all social cost computations were conducted in U.S. dollars, foreign exchange costs were valued at their real dollar value. Local costs, on the other hand, were first converted into U.S. dollars at the official exchange rate and were then multiplied by the shadow foreign exchange factor to arrive at their social U.S. dollar value. Labor costs, power costs, and the local cost component of equipment, spare parts, and buildings were treated in this manner. The cost of capital was considered a foreign exchange cost under the assumption that any marginal increase in the capital available to the country comes from foreign investment or borrowing abroad and that a decrease in capital needs would result in reduced foreign borrowings.

Notes

Chapter 1

1. For definitions and descriptions of unemployment and underemployment in developing countries, see Jacob Viner, "Some Reflections on the Concept of 'Disguised Unemployment,' " in *Contribuicoes a Analise do Desenvoluimenṭo Economico* (Rio de Janeiro: Livraria Agir Editora, 1957); Gottfried Haberler, "Critical Observations of Some Current Notions in the Theory of Economic Development," *L'Industria*, no. 2 (1957).

2. For a description and analysis of these economic characteristics, see Everett E. Hagen, *The Economics of Development* (New York: Irwin, 1968).

3. For a review of government policies and their impact on technology choice, see Shankar N. Acharya, *Fiscal/Financial Intervention, Factor Prices and Factor Proportions: A Review of Issues*, Staff Working Paper No. 183 (Washington, D.C.: World Bank, 1974).

4. For a systematic investigation of the possible motivations of U.S.-based firms to adapt their products and processes to the needs of developing countries, see Robert B. Stobaugh, *The Inducement of U.S. Firms to Adapt Products and Processes to Meet Conditions in Less-Developed Countries*, report to AID, mimeographed (Boston: Harvard Business School, June 1976).

5. This study will not attempt to make a comprehensive review of the literature on technology choice. It will refer to other studies only for the purpose of comparing findings or shedding additional light on some questions raised.

6. For studies looking at specific steps in the production process and separating processing and handling steps, see Louis T. Wells, "Economic Man and Engineering Man," and Howard Pack, "The Substitution of Labor for Capital in Kenyan Manufacturing."

7. See, for an example of an exception, Howard Pack, "The Optimality of Used Equipment: Calculations for the Cotton Textile Industry."

8. See "Statistics on Science and Technology," in *UNESCO Statistical Yearbook* (1974).

9. International Federation of Cotton and Allied Textile Industries, *International Cotton Industry Statistics*, vol. 17 (1974).

10. Raymond Vernon, *Sovereignty at Bay* (New York: Basic Books, 1971), pp. 14–15.

11. Ibid.

Chapter 2

1. These results are not surprising for the textile industry where several other studies have reached the same conclusion. See, for example, Howard Pack, "The Choice of Technique in Cotton Textiles"; James Pickett and R. Robson, "Technology and Employment in the Production of Cotton Cloth"; United Nations Industrial Development Organization, "Technological and Economic Aspects of Establishing Textile Industries in Developing Countries." They are more unexpected for the pulp and paper industry since this industry is classified as a chemical process industry. While a high level of technological fixity in chemical process industries is often assumed (see, for example, James Keddie, "Adoption of Production Technique by Industrial Firms in Indonesia," and Gerard Boon, *Economic Choice of Human and Physical Factors in Production*), very few studies have in fact been done of the scope for capital labor substitution in these industries.

2. George E. Linton, *Natural and Manmade Textile Fibers: Raw Material to Finished Fabric* (New York: Duell, Sloan and Pearce, 1966), lists twenty-seven wet finishing treatments, eighteen dry finishing treatments, and thirty-one protective or special treatments and finishes.

3. For more detailed technical information on the textile production process, see ibid. and UNIDO, "Technological and Economic Aspects."

4. For more detailed information on the pulp and paper production processes, see Robert R. A. Higham, *A Handbook of Papermaking* (London: Business Books Limited, 1969), and his *A Handbook of Paperboard and Board* (London: Business Books Limited, 1970).

5. The ranking of these technologies roughly follows the categorization proposed by James R. Bright. See James R. Bright, *Automation and Management*, p. 45.

Chapter 3

1. For a definition and an example of the use of technology profits, see James R. Bright, *Automation and Management*.

Chapter 4

1. Raymond Vernon, in *Storm over the Multinationals* (Cambridge: Harvard University Press, 1977), p. 55, remarks, "It is contended that, when producing

the same products on the same scale multinational enterprises tend to choose production techniques more capital intensive than those chosen by national firms. . . . But the evidence in support of the conclusion is not very consistent. Some studies support the conclusion, some are inconclusive, and some point to exactly the opposite pattern, suggesting that the subsidiaries of multinational enterprises are more adaptive than their local competitors."

2. Louis T. Wells, Jr., "Economic Man and Engineering Man: Choice of Technology in a Low Wage Country."

3. Yair Aharoni, *The Foreign Investment Decision Process* (Boston: Harvard University Graduate School of Business Administration, Division of Research, 1966), abstract, p. 124.

4. In the future the People's Republic of China might be an important source of such labor-intensive technologies, but at the time of this study, it was not exporting textile equipment except for projects financed by Chinese development aid. Several such projects can be found in Africa.

5. See, for example, Frederick T. Knickerbocker, *Oligopolistic Reaction and Multinational Enterprises* (Boston: Harvard University Graduate School of Business, Division of Research, 1973).

6. Wayne A. Yeoman, "Selection of Production Processes for the Manufacturing Subsidiaries of U.S. Based Multinational Corporations" (D.B.A. thesis, Harvard University, 1968).

7. Similar conclusions were reached by Wells, "Economic and Engineering Man," and David Williams, "Choice of Technology and National Planning: The Case of Tanzania" (D.B.A. thesis, Harvard University, 1976).

8. For a detailed analysis of the structure and impact of the incentives offered to promote the industrialization of northeast Brazil, see David E. Goodman and Roberto Cavalcanti de Albuquerque, *Incentives a Industrializacao e Desenvolvimento do Nordeste* (Rio de Janeiro: IPEA/INPES, 1974).

Chapter 5

1. Figures computed on the basis of national production statistics as reported by *Pulp and Paper International* (1975).

2. For a detailed exposition of the relation between economies of scale and capital intensity in the chemical industry, and a comparison with mechanical industries, see David Felix, "The Technological Factor in Socio-Economic Dualism: Toward an Economy of Scale Paradigm for Development Theory," mimeographed (January 1976).

3. For an evaluation of the 0.6 formula limitations, see Bela Gold, "Evaluating Scale Economies: The Case of Japanese Blast Furnaces," *Journal of Industrial Economics* 23 (September 1974).

Chapter 7

1. For a systematic investigation of the possible motivations of U.S.-based firms to adapt their products and processes to the needs of developing countries, see Robert B. Stobaugh, *The Inducement of U.S. Firms to Adapt Products and Processes to Meet Conditions in Less-Developed Countries*.

2. For a review of government policies and their impact on technology choice, see Shankar N. Acharya, *Fiscal/Financial Intervention, Factor Prices and Factor Proportions: A Review of Issues*.

3. See, for example, Howard Pack, *The Choice of Technique in Cotton Textiles*; James Pickett and R. Robson, *Technology and Employment in the Production of Cotton Cloth*; and UNIDO, *Technological and Economic Aspects of Establishing Textile Industries in Developing Countries* (Vienna: United Nations, 1967).

4. While a high level of technological fixity in chemical process industries is often assumed (see, for example, James Keddie, "Adoption of Production Technique by Industrial Firms in Indonesia" and Gerard Boon, *Economic Choice of Human and Physical Factors in Production*), very few studies have in fact been done of the scope for capital labor substitution in these industries.

5. See, for example, W. Baer and M. Herve, "Employment and Industrialization in Developing Countries"; W. P. Strassman, *Technological Change and Economic Development: The Manufacturing Experience of Mexico and Puerto Rico*; and G. Pfeffermann, *Industrial Labor in the Republic of Senegal*. New York: Praeger, 1968.

6. Their argument is that capital-intensive technologies will help scarce management resources organize and plan for production and will save on skilled labor by substituting machine precision for labor skill and on supervisory skills by reducing the size of the work force. The choice of such capital-intensive technologies, it is argued, should lead to more rapid economic growth. See, for example, Albert O. Hirschman, *The Strategy of Economic Development*, and Wassiley Leontief, *Factors in Economic Development*.

7. Howard Pack, "The Substitution of Labor for Capital in Kenyan Manufacturing."

8. Louis T. Wells, "Economic Man and Engineering Man"; Samuel A. Morley and Gordon W. Smith, *Managerial Discretion and the Choice of Technology by Multinational Firms in Brazil*; and Edward S. Mason, *Promoting Economic Development*.

9. Robert B. Stobaugh et al., *Nine Investments Abroad and Their Impact at Home*.

10. Walter A. Chudson and Louis T. Wells, *The Acquisition of Proprietary Technology by Developing Countries from Multinational Enterprises: A Review of Issues and Policies*.

11. Pack, "Substitution of Labor for Capital."

12. For an analysis of the firm's motivations, see Stobaugh et al., *Nine Investments Abroad and Their Impact at Home*.

13. David Williams, "National Planning and the Choice of Technology: The Case of Textiles in Tanzania."

14. Wells, "Economic Man"; Wayne A. Yeoman, "Selection of Production Processes for the Manufacturing Subsidiaries of U.S. Based Multinational Corporations."

15. This finding is in sharp contrast with those of Wells in Indonesia and of Lecraw in Thailand (Donald J. Lecraw, "Choice of Technology in Low-Wage Countries: The Case of Thailand") as well as with general expectations, which are that firms from other developing countries, more familiar with the environment of low-wage countries, should use more labor-intensive technologies than developed country firms. Although it is difficult to explain this difference without a detailed description of the foreign investors from developing countries interviewed in the other studies, it seems to be due to the minimum scale of production limitation put on the production units to be included in this study. While the other developing country firms interviewed were very large, modern corporations, the other studies might have included a large proportion of smaller, family-run firms, where different members of the family run the various subsidiaries.

16. Chudson and Wells, *Acquisition of Proprietary Technology*, also make a review of the government policies that could be devised to encourage the adoption of labor-intensive technologies in developing countries.

Bibliography

Abernathy, William J., and Townsend, Phillip L. Technology, Productivity and Process Change. Working Paper. Boston: Division of Research, Graduate School of Business Administration, Harvard University, June 1973.

Acharya, Shankar N. *Fiscal/Financial Intervention, Factor Prices and Factor Proportions: A Review of Issues.* World Bank Staff Working Paper No. 183. August 1974.

Arrow, K. J.; Chenery, H. B.; Minhas, B. S.; and Solow, R. M. "Capital-Labor Substitution and Economic Efficiency." *Review of Economics and Statistics* 43 (August 1961): 225–250.

Baer, W., and Herve, M. "Employment and Industrialization in Developing Countries." *Quarterly Journal of Economics* 80 (February 1966): 88–107.

Baranson, Jack. *Industrial Technologies for Developing Economies.* Praeger Special Studies in International Economics and Development. New York: Praeger, 1969.

Baranson, Jack. *Manufacturing Problems in India: The Cummins Diesel Experience.* Syracuse, N.Y.: Syracuse University Press, 1967.

Baranson, Jack. "Transfer of Technical Knowledge by International Corporations to Developing Economies." *American Economic Review* 56 (May 1966): 259–267.

Baudot, Barbara. "Elements in Choice and Adaptation of Technology by Foreign and/or Local Firms in Developing Countries (An Analysis of Six Case Studies)." Mimeographed. October 1974.

Bhalla, A. S. "Investment Allocation and Technical Choice—A Case of Cotton Spinning Techniques." *Economic Journal* 44 (September 1964): 25.

Bhatt, V. V. "Capital Intensity of Industries: A Comparative Study of Certain Countries." *Bulletin of the Oxford University Institute of Statistics* 18 (May 1956): 179–194.

Boon, Gerard K. *Economic Choice of Human and Physical Factors in Production.* Amsterdam: North-Holland, 1964.

Bright, James R. *Automation and Management.* Boston: Division of Research, Graduate School of Business Administration, Harvard University, 1958.

Bruton, Henry J. *Employment Productivity and Import Substitution*. Research Memorandum No. 44. Williamstown, Mass.: Center for Development Economics, Williams College, March 1972.

Bruton, Henry J. "Productivity Growth in Latin America." *American Economic Review* 57 (December 1967): 1099–1116.

Buchanan, N. S. *International Investment and Economic Welfare*. New York, 1965.

Caves, R. 'nternational Corporations: The International Economics of Foreign Investment." *Economica* 38 (February 1971): 1–27.

Chudson, Walter A., and Wells, Louis T. Jr. *The Acquisition of Proprietary Technology by Developing Countries from Multinational Enterprises: A Review of Issues and Policies*. New York: United Nations, ECOSOC, June 1973.

Clague, Christopher K. "Capital-Labor Substitution in Manufacturing in Underdeveloped Countries." *Econometrica* 37 (July 1969): 528–537.

Clague, Christopher K. "The Determinants of Efficiency in Manufacturing Industries in an Underdeveloped Country." *Economic Development and Cultural Change* 18 (January 1970): 188–205.

Cohen, B. *The Role of the Multinational Firm in the Exports of Manufacturers from Developing Countries*. Discussion Paper No. 177. New Haven: Yale Economic Growth Center, May 1973.

Cooper, Charles. "Policy Interventions for Technological Innovation in Less Developed Economies." Mimeographed. April 1976.

Courtney, William H., and Leipziger, Danny M. "Multinational Corporations in LDCs: The Choice of Technology." Mimeographed. October 1973.

Crane, Diana. *An Inter-Organizational Approach to the Development of Indigenous Technological Capabilities: Some Reflections on the Literature*. OECD Development Center. Industry and Technology Occasional Paper No. 3. December 1974.

Disney, Richard, and Aragaw, Hailu. "The Choice of Technology in the Production of Ammonia and Urea." Mimeographed. University of Strathclyde. September 1975.

Dobb, M. H. "A Note on the So Called Degree of Capital Intensity of Investment in Underdeveloped Countries." In *An Economic Theory and Socialism*, London, 1955.

Dobb, M. H. "Second Thoughts on Capital Intensity." In *Review of Economic Studies*, London, 1960.

Eckaus, Richard S. *Appropriate Technologies for Developing Countries*. Washington, D.C.: National Science Foundation, September 1976.

Eckaus, Richard S. "The Factor Proportions Problem in Underdeveloped Areas." *American Economic Review* 45 (September 1955): 539–565.

Fei, J., and Ranis, G. "Innovation, Capital Accumulation, and Economic Development." *American Economic Review* 53 (June 1963): 283–305.

Fitchett, Delbert A. "Capital-Labor Substitution in the Manufacturing Sector of Panama." *Economic Development and Cultural Change* (April 1976): 577–592.

Galensen, W., and Liebenstein, H. "Investment Criteria, Productivity, and Economic Development." *Quarterly Journal of Economics* (August 1955).

Giral, Jose B. *Esquema Metodologico Para La Documentation de Casas con Exito en La Transferencia, Adaptacion y Desarrollo de Tecnologia Quimica Apropiada (Con seis Ejemplos Reales)*. Washington, D.C.: Organization of American States General Secretariat, January 1975.

Goodman, Louis J. *Appropriate Technology Study: Some Background Concepts, Issues, Examples and Recommendations*. Washington, D.C.: USAID, April 1976.

Hagan, Everett E. *The Economics of Development*. New York: Irwin, 1968.

Hawrylyshyn, Oli. "Biases towards Capital-Intense Techniques and the Employment Problems in LDCs." Mimeographed. September 1975.

Hawrylyshyn, Oli. "The Causes of Underemployment in Development Economics, Some Micro-Analytic Clarifications." Mimeographed. Institute for Economic Research. May 1975.

Higgins, Benjamin. *Economic Development Principles, Problems and Policies*. New York: W. W. Norton, 1959.

Hirschman, Albert O. *The Strategy of Economic Development*. New Haven: Yale University Press, 1958.

Hoffmann, Lutz, and Weber, Bernhard. *Economies of Scale, Factor Intensities and Substitution: Micro Estimates for Malaysia's Manufacturing Industries*. Discussion Paper No. 57. Universitat Regensburg, June 1975.

India. *Report of the Powerloom Enquiry Committee*. New Delhi: Ministry of Industry, May 1964.

Kahn, A. E. "Investment Criteria in Development Programs." *Quarterly Journal of Economics* (February 1951).

Katz, J. *Production Functions, Foreign Investment, and Growth*. Amsterdam: North Holland Publishing Co., 1969.

Keddie, James. "Adoptions of Production Techniques by Industrial Firms in Indonesia." Ph.D. dissertation, Harvard University, 1975.

Keddie, James, and Cleghorn, William. *Brewing in Poor Countries*. David Livingstone Institute of Overseas Development Studies, University of Strathclyde, Strathclyde, U.K.: November 1975.

Lecraw, Donald J. "Choice of Technology in Low-Wage Countries: The Case of Thailand." Ph.D. dissertation, Harvard University, May 1976.

Leff, N. *The Brazilian Capital Goods Industry, 1929–1969*. Cambridge: Harvard University Press, 1968.

Leontief, Wassiley. "The Economic Impact." In Editors of *Scientific American*, *Automatic Control*. New York: Simon and Schuster, 1955.

Leontief, Wassiley. *Factors in Economic Development*. London: George Allen and Unwin, 1962.

Lewis, W. A. *Economic Development with Unlimited Supplies of Labour*. Manchester: Manchester School, May 1954.

McBain, Norman S. *The Choice of Technique in Footwear Manufacture*. University of Strathclyde, December 1975.

McBain, Norman S., and Pickett, James. "Low Cost Technology in Ethiopian Footwear Production." Mimeographed. N.d.

Mason, Edward S. *Promoting Economic Development*. Claremont, Calif.: Claremont College Press, 1955.

Mason, R. Hal. "The Relative Factor Proportions in Manufacturing: A Pilot Study Comparing U.S. Owned Subsidiaries and Local Counterparts in the Philippines." Discussion paper. USAID, Office of Program and Policy Coordination, May 1969.

Mason, R. Hal. *The Transfer of Technology and the Factor Proportions Problem: The Philippines and Mexico*. UNITAR research report no. 10. New York: UNITAR, 1971.

Mason, R. Hal, and Sakong, Il. "Level of Economic Development and Capital-Labor Ratios in Manufacturing." *Review of Economics and Statistics* 53 (May 1971): 176–178.

Morawetz, David. "Employment Implications of Industrialization in Developing Countries: A Survey." *Economic Journal* 84 (September 1974).

Morawetz, David. "Import Substitution, Employment, and Foreign Exchange in Colombia: No Cheers for Petrochemicals." in C. Peter Timmer et al. *The Choice of Technology in Developing Countries (Some Cautionary Tales)*. Harvard Studies in International Affairs, no. 32. Cambridge: Center for International Affairs, Harvard University, 1975.

Morley, Samuel A., and Smith, Gordon W. "Limited Search and the Technology Choices of Multinational Firms in Brazil." *Quarterly Journal of Economics* 91 (May 1977): 263–287.

Morley, Samuel A., and Smith, Gordon W. "The Choice of Technology: Multinational Firms in Brazil." Paper no. 58. Houston, Texas: Program of Development Studies, William Marsh Rice University, Fall 1974.

Morley, Samuel A., and Smith, Gordon W. "Managerial Discretion and the Choice of Technology by Multinational Firms in Brazil." Paper no. 56. Houston, Texas: Program of Development Studies, William Marsh Rice University, Fall 1974.

Netherlands Economic Institute. *The Economics of Mill versus Handloom Weaving in India*. Rotterdam, September 1956.

Pack, Howard, "An Appraisal of Current Knowledge about Existing Appropriate Production Technology." Mimeographed. April 1977.

Pack, Howard. "The Substitution of Labor for Capital in Kenyan Manufacturing." mimeo, published as "Employment and Productivity in Kenyan Manufacturing." *Eastern Africa Economic Review*, Vol. 4, No. 2. December 1972.

Pack, Howard. "The Choice of Technique in Cotton Textiles." Mimeographed. January 1974.

Pack, Howard. "The Optimality of Used Equipment: Calculations for the Cotton Textile Industry." *Economic Development and Cultural Change* 26 (January 1978): 307–325.

Pack, Howard. "Employment in Kenyan Manufacturing—Some Microeconomic Evidence." Mimeographed. April 1972.

Pack, H., and Todaro, M. *Industrialization, Employment, and the Choice of Technology*. Discussion Paper No. 25. Yale Economic Growth Center, September 1970.

Pakistan, Government of. *Report of the Fact-Finding Committee on Handlooms*. Karachi: Ministry of Industries, Government of Pakistan, 1956.

Pickett, James; Forsyth, D. J. C.; and McBain, N. S. "The Choice of Technology, Economic Efficiency and Employment in Developing Countries." *World Development* 2 (March 1974): 47–54.

Pickett, James, and McBain, Norman S. *The Choice of Technology, Industrial Location and Developed Country Adjustment Policy*. University of Strathclyde, n.d.

Pickett, James, and Robson, R. *Technology and Employment in the Production of Cotton Cloth*. University of Strathclyde, n.d.

Polak, J. J. "Balance of Payments Problems of Countries Reconstructing with the Help of Foreign Loans." *Quarterly Journal of Economics* (February 1963).

Ranis, Gustav. *Some Observations on the Economic Framework for Optimum LDC Utilization of Technology*. Yale University Center discussion paper no. 152. Economic Growth Center, August 1972.

Sakong, Il. "Factor Market Price Distortions and Choice of Production Techniques in Developing Countries." Ph.D. dissertation, University of California, 1969.

Sen, A. K. *Choice of Techniques: An Aspect of the Theory of Planned Economic Development*. Oxford: Basil Blackwell, 1960.

Sen, A. K. "Choice of Technology: A Critical Survey of a Class of Debates." In *Planning for Advanced Skills and Technologies*. Industrial Planning and Programming Series no. 3. New York: United Nations, 1969.

Singer, Hans W. "Problems of Industrialization of Underdeveloped Countries." *International Social Science Bulletin* 6 (1954).

Stern, Joseph J. *The Employment Impact of Industrial Investment: A Preliminary Report*. Cambridge: Harvard Institute for International Development, Harvard University, January 1977.

Stewart, Francis. "Choice of Technique in Developing Countries." *Journal of Development Studies* 9 (October 1972).

Stewart, Francis. "Technology and Employment in Less Developed Countries." Mimeographed. 1973.

Stobaugh, Robert B. *The Inducement of U.S. Firms to Adapt Products and Processes to Meet Conditions in Less-Developed Countries.* Washington, D.C.: A Report to USAID, June 1976.

Stobaugh, Robert B. *The International Transfer of Technology in the Establishment of the Petrochemical Industry in Developing Countries.* New York: UNITAR, 1971.

Stobaugh, Robert B., et al. *Nine Investments Abroad and Their Impact at Home.* Boston: Division of Research, Graduate School of Business Administration, Harvard University, 1976.

Strassman, W. *Technological Change and Economic Development: The Manufacturing Experience of Mexico and Puerto Rico.* Ithaca, N.Y.: Cornell University Press, 1968.

Strathclyde, University of. *Guidelines for Product Studies in the Appropriate Technology Research Project.* David Livingstone Institute of Overseas Development Studies. October 1974.

Strathclyde, University of. *A Report on a Pilot Investigation of the Choice of Technology in Developing Countries.* David Livingstone Institute of Overseas Development Studies. December 1975.

Timmer, C. Peter. "The Choice of Technique in Indonesia." in Peter Timmer et al. *The Choice of Technology in Developing Countries (Some Cautionary Tales).* Harvard Studies in International Affairs no. 32. Cambridge: Center for International Affairs, Harvard University, 1975.

Uhlig, S. J., and Bhat, B. A. *The Choice of Technique in Maize Milling.* University of Strathclyde, February 1976.

UNIDO. *Technological and Economic Aspects of Establishing Textile Industries in Developing Countries.* United Nations Industrial Development Organization, Vienna: United Nations, 1967.

Wells, Louis T. "Economic Man and Engineering Man: Choice of Technology in a Low Wage Country." In Peter Timmer et al., *The Choice of Technology in Developing Countries.* Harvard Studies in International Affairs 32. Cambridge: Center for International Affairs, Harvard University, 1975.

Westphal, Larry; Joon, Woo Nam; and Rhee, Yung Whee, *Data Development for a Study of the Scope for Capital-Labor Substitution in the Mechanical Engineering Industries.* Washington, D.C.: World Bank, February 1973.

Westphal, Larry E., and Rhee, Yung W. "A Micro, Econometric Investigation of the Impact of Industrial Policy on Technology Choice." Paper presented at the Econometric Society Meetings, Atlantic City, September 1976.

White, Lawrence J. *Appropriate Technology and a Competitive Environment—Some Evidence from Pakistan.* Research Program in Economic Development,

Woodrow Wilson School of Public and International Affairs. Discussion paper no. 46. Princeton, N.J., May 1974.

White, Lawrence J. "Appropriate Technology, X-Inefficiency, and a Competitive Environment: Some Evidence from Pakistan." *Quarterly Journal of Economics* 90 (November 1976): 575–589.

Williams, David. "Choice of Technology and National Planning: The Case of Tanzania." D.B.A. thesis, Harvard University, 1976.

World Bank. *Scope for the Substitution of Labor and Equipment in Civil Construction: A Progress Report.* Washington, D.C.: World Bank, July 1976.

Yeoman, Wayne A. "Selection of Production Processes for the Manufacturing Subsidiaries of U.S. Based Multinational Corporations." Ph.D. dissertation, Harvard University, 1968.

Young, Earl Cross. "An Analysis of Factors Influencing the Decision to Adopt Changes in Production Technology in Selected Chemical Firms in Mexico and Colombia." Ph.D. dissertation, Northwestern University, 1972.

Index